"Yes. Finally a book that explores the complexities of guilt, insecurity, love, compassion, reflection, and resilience. Your nakedness had me in tears. The words on the page scream gratitude and acceptance. We want the ultimate life spree; this is the blueprint to do the work. Thank you, Kate, for sharing your journey and pivot with us in *Believe It and Behave It: How to Restart, Reset, and Reframe Your Life*."

Karen Taylor-Bass
PR Expert and Bestselling Author
KarenTaylorBass.com

"*Believe It and Behave It: How to Restart, Reset, and Reframe Your Life* is a must-read for anyone who is facing or has faced a crisis. Kate's honest, powerful, and timeless wisdom revives the human spirit and reaffirms with grace, humor, and love that we were each here for a reason. And more than anything, we matter."

Theresa Campbell
Founder of Her Life, Her Legacy Leadership and Listening Institute for Women
HerLifeHerLegacy.com

"Have you ever realized that the worst things that happened to you were intended to inspire others? In her debut book, *Believe It and Behave It: How to Restart, Reset, and Reframe Your Life*, Kate Harvie tells her story of discovering joy after an appointment with disaster. Humorous, thoughtful, and practical, Kate's book will cause you to take a second look at finding the fortune in unfortunate events."

Justin Foster
Co-Founder of Root + River, Speaker, Author

"Starting over can be scary. When you're letting go of *who* you once were and *what* life once was, it can be a vulnerable and lonely time navigating the negative self-talk. *Believe It and Behave It: How to Restart, Reset, and Reframe Your Life* is a book about hope and resilience. Kate Harvie's story is not only jaw-dropping and inspiring because she cheated death and learned how to rebuild her life, the wisdom she shares will help you understand that you are not alone – and, most importantly, you already are enough."

Berni Xiong
Author of *The Year of the Brave Bear* and
The Way of the Brave Bear
Contributing author of *Chicken Soup for the Soul: Time to Thrive*
BerniXiong.com

BELIEVE IT AND BEHAVE IT

How to Restart, Reset, and Reframe Your Life

KATE HARVIE

Printed in the United States of America

Published by Author Academy Elite
P.O. Box 43, Powell, OH 43035

www.AuthorAcademyElite.com

Paperback ISBN-13: 978-1-64085-120-7

Hardcover ISBN-13: 978-1-64085-123-8

eBook ISBN-13: 978-1-64085-125-2

Library of Congress Control Number: 2017914466

To everyone who has started from scratch,
Who wants to start from scratch, and
Who *has* to start from scratch,

You've got this.

To my family and FFLFR
With appreciation, admiration, and love,

Thank you.

CONTENTS

INTRODUCTION

Hi, and thank you for choosing to read my book.

While that may seem like a juvenile way to begin your experience, I do really thank you for taking the time to pick up this volume. You may have seen the title and enjoyed the alliteration. You may have read the subtitle and thought, "This could be useful for me because I'm dealing with a whole lotta stuff right now."

Whatever your reason is, thank you.

As you read, you'll see how expressive I am. I'm appreciative and I'm accountable. For the most part, I wrote this the way that I talk. I want to connect with you, not dictate to you.

A few things to remember:

- These are not directions or guidelines to you, the reader.
- Feel free to skip what you feel doesn't apply to you; while my intent is to help you, you know what you need.

Please do not feel sorry for me (why I say this will be clear when you read the first chapter); terrible things can happen to any of us.

We deal. We cope. We grow.

What's the story with this book's title – *Believe It and Behave It*?

A couple of years ago, the idea of manifesting was a frequent topic in various communities and industries. I read about it. I heard talks about it. And I found a way to do it that makes sense to me.

When something I want seems unattainable, to make it happen I **Believe it**, and then I **Behave it**.

This is the opposite of faking it until you make it.

By *believing* it, you know it is in progress. Perhaps it's happening at a slower pace than you might want, but it is happening.

By *behaving* it, you operate as though you are in action: you introduce yourself, dress like, and discuss things like the person you are on the verge of becoming.

There is no faking it, because you are *actually* making it. It just isn't being made out loud, obviously, or for the sake of anyone but yourself.

So, why did I write this book?

You're reading it so I want to share my reasons with you.

If I survived something that, according to those who know, was supposed to have killed me, and I continue to hold my place in the world, I survived for reasons beyond the medical teams' efforts and people's prayers.

Had I dealt with certain things differently (and better) over the last eight years, who knows what could have happened? Actually, I do know, and that is why I wrote this book. I am as candid here as I can be, using my truest voice and hoping to help others. I use all the truth I now have so I can share the knowledge I lacked immediately and sometime after being hurt.

If I am to have the privilege (and it *is* a privilege) to take up space in the world, it shall be for at least one significant reason: to give people actionable information to ensure a happier and stronger life, particularly one following a mess, disaster, or crisis.

If I had known a fraction of what I came to learn in recovery and several years after, I could have prevented and managed all kinds of things (some of which I call post-trauma trauma) so much better. If it didn't go sideways in my life, it may as well not have happened.

During my official recovery and my "unofficial" (2010 until late 2014) recovery, more often than not, I did indeed...

- Hate myself
- Regret pretty much everything.
- Contribute considerably to the destruction of relationships
- Spend money on things (and sometimes people) that defined "sunk cost"
- Act desperate under the guise of appearing eager.

I may as well not have been alive.

One of my reasons for being is to provide actionable truths to people. Truths and tactics. When we believe, trust, and apply them, they can help us to feel happier and less doubtful.

We are worth having, and living, **a life that is powered by happiness, clarity, and truth.** Our divine rights include being happy first and most often, especially if things were once (or are) messed up in our worlds.

Our world is better this way: feel happy first and love ourselves first. You first. Me first. Us first. That is the world in which I want all of us to live.

That's my why.

If you have any questions or need clarity and you don't want to wait until you're finished with the book, jump to the Appendix in the back where you will see my website and email address.

1

HOW IT ALL BEGAN

February 12th, 2009 began with a combination of the expected – my oldest godson's birthday – and the unexpected – I'd been laid off from a job a week earlier, interviews weren't happening until the following week, and I was going to spend the day with a friend.

At my friend's home in Brooklyn, we discussed hair color and she commented that she liked mine. I remembered that my hair stylist charged less when she did services at home, so I called her to see if she was available. She *was* and she was happy to color my friend's hair. I got the address, and off we walked.

I don't remember anything else until a day in late March of that year when I woke up and my brother, Ted, who lived in the Boston area, was sitting next to my bed.

I smiled and said, "Hi. What's up?"

Ted asked me if I knew where I was. I looked around and I think I said, "I'm not at home."

I wasn't at home. I was in Mount Sinai Hospital in New York City. This was the second hospital in which I had been; I had been at NYU Lutheran Medical Center[1] in Brooklyn from February 12th until March 2nd.

While my friend and I were walking to my hair stylist's home, we crossed one of many streets. While I was on the crosswalk, retrieving my hat that the wind had blown off my head, I was hit by an ambulette. Ironic?

I suffered what is medically called a traumatic brain injury. I only know how it happened and what follows because people told me. The ambulette hit me so hard that I was knocked down the street. I sustained multiple skull fractures and contusions to my brain. I went into a coma soon after that and remained comatose for two and a half weeks. There was concern that I would not wake up.

The brain swelling increased my intracranial pressure, which was potentially life-threatening, so surgeons removed a portion of my skull. The pressure did subside to what was considered normal levels and my recovery conditions improved. To address a subdural hematoma, I had a frontoparietal temporal craniectomy shortly after arriving at Lutheran. Around two weeks later, respiratory failure required mechanical ventilation so I had a tracheotomy and an intravenous filter implant.

At Mount Sinai's neurosurgery unit I underwent a cranioplasty that placed a synthetic bone flap on my skull and a ventriculoperitoneal shunt to treat my excess cerebrospinal fluid. When I arrived at Sinai's inpatient rehabilitation, my cognition was so devastatingly disrupted that I could not speak. I was disoriented and confused. I could not retain information from minute to minute. My cognition was so

---

[1] This hospital is now called NYU Langone Hospital – Brooklyn.

poor that I required a sitter to be with me 24 hours a day so I would not be a risk to myself. While my cognition improved considerably during my in-patient experience, it was still severely impaired when I was discharged.

When I left Mount Sinai my memory abilities, compared to women my age, were below the 1st percentile. That level of performance is similar to what would be seen in an intellectually disabled person. I was hospitalized until April 25th, 2009. Four days later, I went to Ohio where I would live with my parents until September.

I share the details about my surgeries, my brain, and what my condition was eight years ago to give you context.

Context: A set of circumstances that surround a particular event or situation.

I want you to have context when you look through (and hopefully read) this book.

After I was hurt, I rebuilt, reset, and reframed everything I could so I would wake up each day and be.

Be what exactly?

Be hopeful.
Be active.
Be happy.

You are likely a soldier in your own right, struggling to pick up the pieces from loss, trauma, letdown, destruction. You may have recovered, remade, and restarted too. If so, I tip my hat to you. I could learn a lot from you and I know it. I appreciate you taking a look at these pages.

Again, thank you.

Note

My life has been like a game of Chutes and Ladders since February 12th, 2009, and through all of those ups and downs, I have learned some things.

To share those with you, I designed a framework that uses specific experiences to tell you how I felt, what I did, and what I learned.

In my parlance, they break down to **React, Act, Fact.**

Those appear on the first page of chapters 2 through 14.

2

STARTING FROM SCRATCH – MAKING SENSE OF THAT (OR TRYING TO)

React:
Unclear, confused, and sad. Frequently. Oh, who are we kidding? Always.
Act:
Ask questions. Feel ashamed and weak every single time you ask anything.
Fact:
There is no shame in ANY part of your game.

When I was living at my parents' house, it initially seemed to be an awesome and perfect setup: I was really thin, didn't go to work every day, and had no obligations to sweat. In theory, this was really, really good. It just didn't feel that way.

You see, I was used to being busy. My life was fairly full between a job, volunteer work, seeing friends, going to shows, dating (not much though it bears mentioning), and just being out and about in the city I'd made my home since I was a grown woman (which, by my measurement, began in December, '99).

While this would have been altogether different had I not been hurt, having been downsized on February 5th, 2009, it wouldn't have been that different...because I wouldn't have been different.

By this point, pretty much everyone in the US had experienced something tough that was work-related, due to the burst of the real estate bubble and the economy's reaction. When I was laid off, I figured I'd quickly find another job. I would have continued to manage my contractor (hired by me to renovate my apartment). I'd get healthier (translation: lose weight). I would go on living what I referred to as "the life" in *my* NYC.

None of that was to happen.

So I went to the drawing board. I tried to figure out what the heck to do, and how in the hell to exist, in the time the universe had blessedly granted me post-accident.

Trust that there wasn't much I could do. I wrote around 130 thank you notes to those who had kindly showed up for my family and me. (If I needed to write you and you didn't receive one, please know how much I appreciate you. I'm sorry and thank you!)

Doing what I could to acclimate to my parents' house (where I hadn't spent much time as it wasn't our childhood home), I got to know every space that I could claim inside and outside. Because I couldn't drive (pending the taking of (and passing!) a souped-up Driver's Ed course), I felt dependent upon those who could and were willing to drive me someplace or meet me where I was staying. To say that I felt like I was burdening these folks is an understatement.

I taught myself to ask for help. Rather, I told myself I was doing that.

Growing up as I did, when I did, and coming up how and when I did, you just didn't ask for help. It was a sign of weakness. You sucked. You weren't capable. You were stupid. Straight up, you were a failure. It was bad enough that I was without a job, not earning money, not living in the home I had put together.

On top of all this, I couldn't make things happen or remember things as simple as what had happened three months ago. Whether it was my ego acting up or just what was so foreign to me, I struggled silently and said to myself over and over again, "You will figure all of this out. Time takes time. You're still healing," and on and on and on. I didn't believe any of it.

So why didn't I put down my Wonder Woman bracelets and tiara and just say, "Help?!"
Because I had *actual*, real survivor guilt.

To my knowledge, actual survivor guilt doesn't exist. I heard the term "survivor guilt" from a neuropsychologist I saw once I returned home to New York. This effect had nothing to do with me; it was likely felt, according to him, by the friend who had been with me the day I was hurt. (More on that later.)

Actual survivor guilt is–for lack of a better term–what a person who survived the trauma can feel when he or she comes out of the traumatic experience. It's not that the people who were with them during that nightmare experience have any less of a right to feel empty and scared. Actual survivor guilt feels shameful and selfish, both of which add to the post-trauma recovery in initially deceptive and ultimately damaging ways.

How dare I ask for anything when, dammit, it was my privilege to walk on this Earth? I felt terrible when:

- I couldn't remember the names of people I'd known since age 5.
- I had no job and no way to make money.
- As thin as I'd been during my first year of law school, there was no one to appreciate it or give me the eye.
- The wigs I'd bought may as well have been styled for a Carol Channing impersonator. So I was either going to be bald for the world to see or master the tying of do-rags or babushkas.

And, I was alive.

Any complaints or frustrations were beneath me. I had survived an injury that, were it not for the exceptional team at Lutheran Medical, prayers and support for and from family, friends, and colleagues, was supposed to have killed me.

Asking for help was not going to happen. The people who loved me had been through enough. Add to that, it was not natural for me to ask others for anything, let alone assistance. "Take care of you." That's what Gen X does well.

What I forgot—or chose not to remember—is **people who solve problems for a living in various capacities**, which I did (and do), **tend to make things that are not that tricky more difficult**. So much of what upset and frustrated me in the months following my release from the hospital was not serious.

Because I was scared (understatement) by the unfamiliar, the forgotten, and the yet to be, I distracted myself from this by twisting things. Someone who coined the term "manufactured drama" with their brother friend ought to have recognized this. Right?

It didn't matter that I didn't remember how to scramble eggs. No one cared about me failing to remember who directed movies in the 70s and 80s.
The distance from my parents' house to the mall was covered with the help of GPS.
People's names stayed the same; reintroducing myself would restore that information.

I am not made weak by stating I cannot do something. What would happen if I didn't learn how to do it? Go through life in a fog of fear, regret, and insecurity.

It certainly began that way when I was in what I call "official" recovery. Not only did I not want to burden anyone to do even more for me, I expected myself to wake up, stand up, and show up. Every day. Without pause.

Time goes so fast now. A minute is a day, a week is a month, a month is a lifetime.

Being off the grid for eight months was akin to me holing up in a cave without web access or phone service. People's attention spans (and memories) are becoming shorter and smaller. I felt it was only a matter of time before people forgot me. My value to the world was diminishing.

It wasn't enough that I was alive. There was supposed to be more.

Where were my creations and contributions?
What about my presence? - my being somewhere with people to help, write, strategize, edit, market, support, and love. I didn't feel I was worth the time and energy spent by people to tolerate me.
What could I bring to *any* environment?

I often say that no one is a stronger critic of me than me. That is for sure and certain the truth.

When I set unreachable expectations for myself, what was I doing but making a path to and voluntarily stepping into quicksand? **Was I, am I, not worth a minute to process what is *really* going on in the world, in *my* world?**

It's not as though I owed people favors and had to pay them back for being kind to my family, hoping I'd wake up, knowing I'd one day be "me." Every single person who prayed, visited me in the hospital, drove my mother to IKEA did so because they wanted to, not because they were obligated.

The only person who *had* to do anything in this situation was me. So, **what I had to do was love myself completely in the ways I love others**: wholeheartedly, from the top to the bottom, all the quirks and foibles, as they are right fucking now.

What I did not realize was that I had also contributed to my survival. Coming out of the two and half week coma wasn't just because the world wasn't finished with me; **I wasn't done with the world**.

There was, there is still, and there always will be no shame in my game. Never. Ever.

3

TIME AS A GIFT AND TIME AS A TEST

React:
Albert Einstein said it: "The definition of insanity is doing things the same way and expecting different results." What has worked in the past will not work again if you want different results. It's time to turn everything over.
Act:
When all you have is time, you do things to fill it. You do as much as you can, however you can, whenever you can. Do. Do. Do. Fast. Quickly. Like your life depends on it.
Fact:
It is a gift to have the time to experience things. Know that you can take that time to process and learn, to find and apply better ways to be.

Having loads of time without obligations and expectations can be a gift.

It can also be a black hole when you're a self-starter. When you're accustomed to having things to do and responsibilities and activities, being unoccupied can feel like a mystery you can't solve. When you have no idea who you are, and what you are, it can be something of a disaster.

Not to overdramatize, and that describes four and a half months of my life in 2009. If I am going to be super honest with you, these things describe 17 months of my life. It wasn't until late December 2010 that I felt I was back. To a degree, that is.

Back from what?

Back *to* what?

Let me start at the very beginning. (If only this was as easy as "Do Re Mi." Points for all the super fans of *The Sound of Music*.)

Two days, if memory serves, before my release from the second hospital I stayed in after my injury, I was called into a meeting with the lead neurologist and various staff who had worked on my case. (Things sound better when you use the vernacular of Sherlock Holmes.) During this meeting, I learned from the doctor that New York law dictates it is illegal to live alone when you're released from medical care for an injury such as mine.

Come again?

This knowledge was dropped when I was asked where I live. The sarky side of me, which was a defense mechanism operating at full force, wanted to say, "You have my records in front of you and my address is there." I told the doctor my logistical coordinates. He asked if I had roommates. With relief I told him, no, I did not. He went on to let me know that I would not be living there for the foreseeable future.

I suffered the sort of neurological trauma that placed me in the previously mentioned legal category. As a result, there would be no return to my apartment that had been under renovation since November 2008. I was no longer going to step into what I had believed was my grown-up semi-Barbie dream house residence.

Before I could ask where on Earth I was to go, the doctor told me my parents were going to house me.

Come again, again?

My parents had attended a meeting immediately prior to mine. I didn't know they were in town (they live in Ohio). And I absolutely didn't know that I would be leaving the hospital to "recover" further at their house.

Here's where things got awkward.

I'm not someone who feels entitled. I am grateful for everyone and everything in my life (even more so during my recovery). I know I was lucky, blessed, whatever you want to call it, that the company who'd laid me off on February 5th hadn't dotted all the I's and crossed all the T's so I was still under their health insurance when I was hurt.

I know I was even luckier and more blessed to the umpteenth power of whatever you believe in that my parents had space for me at their house and that they were willing to board me for as long as it took for me to be considered healthy enough to live on my own again.

Still, despite all this, I wanted to be by myself and put myself back together.

That is what I knew: take care of me.
Be who I am.
Do things how I know.

None of those were to be so.

Thus, I began a time in my life where pretty much everything I thought and most of what I did differed from who I was and what I needed at the time. How we learn – or one of the ways we can learn – is by doing things. I tapped into my kinesthetic self, powered by fear, hurt, ignorance, and shame, acting like I knew what I was doing.

Does that sound or feel familiar?

I invite you to come down the rabbit hole with me. We will get into what I felt, did, and learned during my "official" recovery time. My clinical hypnotherapist, the incomparable Karla Lightfoot, reminded a group of us during an event in January 2017 that **the subconscious does not know fact from fiction**. I don't know if realizing that would have been useful during this most challenging time in my life, but it should be said it has since become one of the most important concepts and truths applied to my life. I hope it will be helpful for you, too.

Once I arrived at my parents' house in Ohio (driven there by a dear friend in a rented minivan), I tried to settle into the environment. This was not the house my brother and I had grown up in. The longest I had ever stayed there was five months in 1999. I had lived by myself in New York City since December 1999, other than two years in St. Louis. I would not, or could not, see my parents' home as anything more than a house that was assigned to me.

It was a punishment. I was being sentenced because I was weak, messed up, all but destroyed, and lucky to be alive. It was not my place; it was not my space.

With that as my mindset, I pushed, pulled, and endeavored to make this place just like my home in terms of behaviors and routines. I believed that you can make any place your home when you surround yourself with the people, experiences, and activities that resonate with you most.

One of the things I learned when I worked at Sephora US in Education was the value of the plus/delta model: positive attributes paralleled with negative ones. Early in my Ohio sentence, I drew up a list of plusses and deltas about my forthcoming experience. As a believer in and applier of (or so I thought) positive psychology, I knew intellectually that plusses *can* always outweigh the deltas. If the deltas outweigh the plusses, the universe is telling you there are things to be learned.

What I did not realize is that you need context, a useful framework, and the straight-up desire to be consistently happy with the plus/delta-ing of your life to yield good things.

So there I am, bald as a baby and skinny as a rail (which was something of a joy for me as sustaining a lean frame had always been a challenge), and I made a list of all of the things that sucked:

- I was not allowed to drive my car.
- Hardly any of my friends lived in Ohio.
- The friends who did live in Ohio were married or partnered, had children, worked full time, and were living active and managed lives.
- I did not have a job (I was laid off one week before I was hurt).

- I was not involved with any not-for-profits or charitable organizations.
- I wasn't dating anyone (which was actually a good thing and there will be more on this later).
- Pretty much everyone I knew lived a productive life and had not been off grid, paused, and back burnered for three months.

And this list continued, full of significant things and insignificant things.

What I did not realize is when you start from scratch, which is somewhat more challenging when it's not your choice, **everything feels significant.**

Of course, we cannot choose where we are in life when something messed up happens. And, it's safe to say that if you're in a tricky or twisted place when trauma occurs, everything that follows the incident will be somewhat heightened.

In other words, the victim-y feelings can be exacerbated by whatever preceded the trauma. I know that my feelings were. It's important to know this. What I did not realize was that I was vulnerable and scared when the ambulette hit me.

Everything was seasoned by hurt, feelings of disappointment, and the one of the worst villains in one's heart and mind: self-hatred.

What had been going on with me included these things:

- One week before I was hurt, I was laid off from a job I, frankly, no longer enjoyed.

- I was feeling somewhat overwhelmed about turning 35, primarily because I wasn't where I thought I'd be and didn't have what I thought I would have at this age. (Notice that I *thought* these things to be true.)
- For the first time in my life, I shamed myself for being single.
- My claims to focus on the present moment and not dwell on the previous moment or trip on the future moment were only that: claims. There was little to no action behind them.
- My efforts to find positivity in good things, like my apartment renovations, my parents' health and happiness, my excellent brother and his fiancée, were half-assed. Truth.

I was not on my own side as much as I could have been when I was released from the hospital. And I know why this was.

I was not understanding and supportive of myself as I stepped into an unfamiliar place.
I felt weak and self-serving, pathetic and childish.
I was 34 years old.
More than once in my life, I had picked myself up, dusted myself off, and started all over again. (Thank you, Frank Sinatra.) Damned if I was going to depend on anyone other than myself while I recovered.

Thus begins what I felt and how I operated during the five or so years after I was hurt.

You may be thinking, "Whoa. That's a long time to be in recovery." You might be right.

Because I was expected to be, and was identified as being, "better" after four and a half months in Ohio, I returned home to New York. I refer to nearly 60 months following my injury to be my "official recovery" and my "unofficial recovery."

Yes. It did take that long.

In fact, I think I will always feel as though I am getting better. Why? Because that's how grateful I am. That's how much I have to learn. And that's how much I know I don't know.

So let's start at the very beginning: my residence (previously called a "sentence" in this chapter) in Ohio.

The air pressure on flights can make our ears pop. It can also have negative effects on brain injury survivors who have equipment installed under their skulls. A shunt, which ensures my neurons are firing at the right rhythms, was placed at the back of the left side of my brain. So flying was not an option. The previously mentioned wonderful friend drove my mother and me from New York City to Ohio.

If you've never driven this route, believe me when I tell you it's dull, drab, and you're better off spending the money and flying. Only half kidding. The challenge of this trek was not so much that I wasn't driving: it was my first experience of **having nothing but time**. When we have what feels like infinite time, and nothing interesting or creative to occupy our minds, the brain, not knowing fact from fiction, can tell stories. And my brain told hella many stories during those miles on Interstate 80:

- Who was I?

- What was I going to do for the next however many months?
- How was I going to get through the next however many months?
- Why had this happened?
- What had I done in this life, or another, to deserve, cause, or conjure this to happen?

Little did I know that by asking myself these questions, ones that did not have any true or healthy answers, I was planting seeds and laying roots for a fear-based, self-hating bed of thorns that would emerge five months later when I was back in New York and living life.

While I was not necessarily set up for success, I unintentionally unraveled all of the best intentions and positive psychology I had been building in myself for years. Whatever people meant to do, whatever they actually did, whatever I hoped I could make happen, and whatever I was actually capable of and willing to do was a puzzle. This puzzle was a jumble of patterns, shapes, characters, and colors made of different materials and the pieces did not fit. Come hell or high water, I continually tried to fit them, usually to no avail. It sure felt good to try though.

The fuel that powered me until sometime in 2014 was a combination of anxiety and insecurity. This pairing is a powerful substance that relies on adrenaline, not instinct, and is naturally born of fear. It's combustible and dangerous. Why? We don't – or maybe we can't – realize that we are operating on energy that cannot be sustained. Long story short, we will collapse.

From the moment I arrived in Ohio, I was uncertain of everything, unclear about all of it, and unsure how I could get by. Instead of hunkering down and processing what had happened (hit by an ambulette) and where I had been for the last two and a half months (two hospitals, in a coma for two and a half weeks in one of them), I did everything I could to fire on all cylinders.

I had all the time in the world.
I was used to deadlines, due dates, and things needing to happen expeditiously.
I felt as though I had dodged a bullet by surviving what was initially believed to be fatal.

I was so grateful I was *in* the world that I forgot to *be* in the world.

I was. Really and truly. For the foreseeable future. Everything needed to happen quickly, I believed. When it didn't (read: when I couldn't make or do anything quickly or effectively), I became frustrated, scared, and angry. Everything seemed to have an expiration date.

How about getting together with friends from law school I hadn't seen since 1999 or thereabouts? I could surely meet their spouses and their children. We were once close friends. Surely that would pick up again. Of course, things would click between the wife and the kids and me. Or they wouldn't. People do kind things for a number of reasons. It's easy to do things for our friends. The less pure, if you will, reasons include acting on obligation, acting out of guilt, and because someone tells you to.

The cynic in me would like to say that many of my social activities that happened in the summer of 2009 were because of one of the less genuine reasons. What I know is that I was not my realest self. I was surely not who people had known before, or thought they'd known. And, people don't have to spend social time with those they don't like. More to the point, they *won't* spend time with those they don't like. Though that covers people I hadn't really been in touch with for a while, it was another thing with my close friends. I had lived in New York for a third of my life at this point, but I grew up in Cleveland. I went to law school in Cleveland. Surely I could be in Ohio with ease and enjoyment. Some of my closest friends live there.

Couldn't we officially reconnect, catch up, do things together, and share the summer?
Won't I learn about their lives, their accomplishments, and their children?
Don't I meet people easily?
Has there ever been a better time to make new friends?

What I neglected to realize was that in the three months that I'd been off grid (read: in the hospital), **a lot had happened in my friends' lives**. While I knew we can never get back time once it's gone, I did not appreciate just how much things can shift in a short time. People's lives don't tend to pause. Their styles, circles, and priorities constantly shift. When you have nothing but time, few scheduled commitments, and even fewer expectations applied to you, you can hang out with your friends. What else is there?

There is the life that has been in play while you were unaware of anything, except when your next neuropsych appointment was at the hospital.
The life you had not been living since February 11, 2009.
The life that is unknown to everyone, except the person who is living it.

People not being available to talk with you, get coffee, go shopping, go to concerts is not a rejection of you. I didn't remember that. Or more accurately, I had never experienced **what it feels like when your life doesn't operate at the same rhythm as your friends' lives.**

Social media had its first real moment when I was in the hospital. People began to communicate with each other more via Facebook. I wasn't particularly active on Facebook once I was released from the hospital. I'd like to say that was my choice, but it was more because I felt ashamed and scared, worried what people might think, as no one wants to open their browser to learn that someone they thought was dead was actually alive.

While text messages had come to the fore a few years before, there was nothing like the Facebook News Feed. When I learned about people's promotions, engagements, marriages, pregnancies, moves around the country (and world), and accomplishments via Facebook (alongside everyone else), I felt I was being left out of people's stories and joys. This is an example of taking personally something that was not personal. I know some of my friendships were harmed by my overreactions to people sharing news on Facebook instead of directly telling me.

I have since forgiven myself for this, knowing now that **intention and perception don't always align**.

Isn't being alone all of the time evidence of being lonely?
Isn't any guy better than no guy?
I asked myself these questions and provided the wrong answers of "yes" and "of course."

Those incorrect thoughts led me to connecting with and meeting several men via online dating. Three of them became boyfriends (and all of those relationships were full of what corporate trainers call "learning moments"). Four more dates resulted in close friendships. So many "dates." So many things booked on the calendar. So little real, heartfelt interaction that lasted more than a couple of hours, if that. **At a time when the best thing for me was to be by myself, I believed that it made me pathetic to be alone so often.**

I didn't have a paying job.
I wasn't volunteering anywhere.
Those contributed to something new: I felt incomplete.

While I was working out all the time and becoming a better cook, that meant little to nothing in the scheme of things for me at the time. While it wasn't bragging rights or stories for my own telenovela, to go on dates (and eventually be in an exclusive relationship) felt like progress. I told myself it was fun. I told myself I was liked for real reasons. Truth be told, I probably enjoyed tying do-rags, wearing hats, and wearing clothes two sizes smaller than I'd worn before my accident the most.

As the summer continued, I decided (and tried) to focus on the small wins.

My cognitive therapist, an exceptional person, was at the root of this. She let me know that my restored abilities to do everything from drive my car to complete crossword puzzles to doing basic math evinced my development and healing. I felt genuinely hopeful that there was a light at the end of the tunnel.

If only being patient with one's self was as easy as being patient with others.

I know this much: it wasn't speed that could and would get me there. What would get me there were trust, belief, and **time**.

4

THE PERSONAL: TAKING AND MAKING

React:
People abandoned me. I learn about their important news and life changing things – IF I learned them – on Facebook, Instagram, and Twitter. No one called, emailed, or texted. WTF.
Act:
Resent them. Feel neglected and left out. Forget that their lives are their lives. Forget that the pause button wasn't pressed on everyone's life.
Fact:
Know that people are living their lives and you may know nothing about them. You likely have nothing to do with it. That's alright. Share when you want. Just be sure you're living *your* life. Get busy doing that.

Once upon a time, a good wireless signal was the new black.

Not really, and my parents' house is set fairly far back from the street. While they have phones, cable TV, and a WiFi network, in 2009 the mobile phone needed to beg, borrow, or steal to get a signal. Network delays that slow down the social media feed is a true first world problem.

When you feel trapped, lack your usual resources and feel the majority of your skills are missing (or you've convinced yourself that you lack the ability to do things and you're definitely not going to ask anyone for help), you can come to count on the feed. The news feed. The social feed.

The word "feed" was chosen for a reason: we're encouraged to need it for sustenance, to sate our hunger, and to distract us from real stuff. Like how watching the clips from the 2016 Tony Awards (read: *Hamilton*) on YouTube can prevent us from barking at the barista who didn't make our coffee right. Or something like that.

We're human, after all: we seek, crave, and need to know, feel, and consume things that affect our senses.

While I was acclimating to my new home in Ohio, I needed to find ways to fill my time. My mother had kept track of everyone and every place that had sent flowers, cards, food, and the like when I was in hospital. I like to say that I'm a combination of current and classic. As such, I write thank you notes. So in May that year I wrote about 130 notes.

I told myself that I was doing this to let people know how much I appreciated their kind gestures and showing up at the hospitals. In truth, I wrote the notes also because I hoped to resuscitate dormant relationships. I hoped to reconnect with people I had not seen in years. I hoped that my sounding the call that I was back (kind of) would have prompted people to say hi and catch up.

It will not surprise you to learn that nothing happened there.

It's not as though I wrote in the letters, "Omigosh, it would be amazing to be in touch with you (I did write something more formal than that in a note to a once close friend who had cut ties with me in 2003) so please email me and let's talk!"

I had read The Four Agreements by Don Miguel Ruiz a few years before I was hurt. I seemed to have forgotten the one that resonated with me most – ask for what you need – during my first steps into recovery. Why? I have asked myself this question several times. Even though I'm not a licensed attorney, I am almost obsessed with causation and the reasons behind things.

Eventually (and by "eventually" I mean in 2017), I realized that **I sought the company of other people because I truly could not stand to be who I was and how I was at this time.**

As thin as I was (and for me, I was thin) and as "low stress" (read: didn't have to go to work, didn't have to worry about making ends meet) as my life was supposed to be, something was going on. Wasn't it enough to be slim and not have to rush to work and travel for three weeks every month?!

When you define who you are based on *what* you do, you never want to have nothing to do.

Because then, who the heck are you?

Social media both supports this – what you do is who you are – and thwarts this. Before Facebook, Twitter, Instagram, Pinterest, Snapchat, and the like, you could tell your friends or take out an ad in a newspaper or magazine, pay for a digital coverage, etc. when you had news about whatever and whoever. The social channel news feeds activate for and apply to everyone the saying "There's no such thing as bad publicity." Or, as I like to say, "There's never a slow news day when you have Facebook."

I have worked in some form of communications since 1999. You'd think that Facebook would be like a flame to my moth self. Not so much. What I had come to appreciate more than ever was honest to goodness talking with people. By this I mean actively voice to voice, face to face, and not somewhat statically via GChat, IM, and SMS.

After nearly three months of not hanging out with people, I was desperate for it. Hospital stays affect everyone differently. Anything that simply simulated such activities was anathema to me. People announced their promotions, moves, engagements, marriages, pregnancies, book releases, album releases, and latest everything on their Facebook walls. To learn these often intimate things via an online source, and not directly from the person, hurt me.

I took all of this news personally, as though someone was leaving me out, excluding me on purpose. Nothing could have been further from the truth.

I didn't realize and I couldn't believe that people shared their news on Facebook, etc. because it was easy, accessible, and the new normal. I all but rejected Facebook. What did I have to share?

That I wasn't dead?
That my hair would eventually grow back?
That my apartment was available to sublet, furnished?

As lonely as I was, I did not see that I could have started conversations and dialogues with people by asking questions and seeking their opinions. People love to talk, and they love to opine. As far as I was concerned, I may as well not communicate with people if I couldn't hear their voices. It may as well have been called Falsebook. It felt so static. I thought, "If someone has time to post on their wall, they have time to answer the phone. They have time to call me back. They have time to call me!"

Time?
Yes, or so it seemed.
Opportunity?
Who knows? While I thought people were ducking me, they were most likely living their lives.
Actual interest?
Perhaps, and very likely, not.

I didn't allow myself to realize that everyone who wasn't recovering from a traumatic brain injury had things to do, mouths to feed, diapers to change, and goals to reach. **When you're by yourself too much, it can become very easy to think that what *you* know and what *you* do is how things are.** This happens so we can protect ourselves from feeling like the other, someone who is so different than everyone else that there is no place for us.

In other words, your square peg becomes squarer and it becomes even less of a fit. Everywhere.

I did this to myself.

No one flat out rejected me and put a closed sign on life's social door. You may be saying, as I certainly did at the time, "If people knew that you were alive and out of the hospital, would it have hurt them so much to have reached out and say 'How are ya?'" Sure, and some people did. Some people visited. Some people sent things.

But, **because I felt that *I* wasn't enough, nothing anyone did was enough.**

It didn't help that I was far from most of my friends. The friends who live in Ohio had productive and meaningful lives. When people "did" – shared, showed, celebrated – things on social, I felt like everyone had a MetroCard for the New York City subway, except me, and no one loaned me their MetroCard.

Here's the thing: **I didn't ask anyone for their MetroCard.**

I had learned only a portion of what people had given, sacrificed, and dedicated to my family and me when I was in the hospitals. As grateful as I was, I felt extremely guilty and that colored everything I said, did, and felt for at least a couple of years.

I know that I'm a lot. By this I mean a lot to handle, in general, and not just because of my injury. And I had never felt so much a lot until the spring and summer of 2009. How could I expect people to want to talk and spend time with me, especially those who had raced to the first hospital when I was in a coma? **As survivors can do, I rejected what made sense: I created a story that focused on what I did not have, what I could not do, and who I was not in touch with.**

(Therapists didn't count. They were being paid to help me.)

Yes, I had survived. It was up to me to figure out everything and get back on track. Instead, I became resentful, confused, and scared.

How dare people continue to live, make, and experience while I was trying to figure out how to complete the New

York Times' Monday crossword? As it became summer, and I began to meet new people (read: find marginal success in online dating), I felt less like a mess. I created an existence in Ohio on my own terms (as much as I could) where I was as social (or not) as I wanted. When I could drive again and work, I felt better about me. Capabilities were restored. Small wins were evidence that I was better.

When we choose not to interact with people, and we opt not to use the available channels and resources to do this, we shift our relationships. While our reasons – to us, anyway – are good, we've gone static. **The return to active from static can be difficult because things happen in the world, whether you're playing in it or not.**

In our world today, six, seven, eight months is a really long time to be off the grid. Things happen all the time. People use the social channels because they're free, easy, and immediately accessible. While you may not feel as though you have newsworthy things to share, you do: simple things, basic FYIs, the latest album, movie, and book you like. It doesn't have to be impressive or braggy to be worth sharing.

What *you're* doing is important because *you* are doing it.

5

SOCIALIZING, OR "SOCIALIZING"

React:
You can silence or quiet down all of the craziness by spending time with friends. It's the summer and what else do we do?
Act:
Make it a priority (over pretty much everything) to invite people to do things, try to make new friends, reconnect with old friends, hang out with friends. Offer to help, do, and pay. Be loud, be brash, and talk way too much because it's not *distraction* when there is *action*. You're alive, you're here, and isn't that awesome. This is a statement, not a question; a question implies that you don't believe it (which you don't).

Fact:
Real friends know, care about, and believe in you. While things between you and them will change direction and go quiet sometimes, that does not mean they are rejecting you. They are doing and living, and that's what you're supposed to do too.

What do you *really* like to do? Watch football, go shopping, travel to faraway places, turn off your phone and go about your day? What keeps you going? What encourages you to feel optimistic about the day to come?

And, what do I love to do?

Drive. Anywhere.
Cook.
Attend photography exhibitions.
Play Sherlock Holmes/Carmen Sandiego in unfamiliar neighborhoods.
Go to the movies (with a hidden hoagie).
Experience live music.
Hang out with friends.

While the preceding list is not in a fixed order, it kind of is. Spending time with friends has always been an important part of my life. It became even more so when I lived in Ohio in the spring and summer of 2009. When I was able to look back on these months with clarity, I realized why this ironic thing – being someone who has always liked to be by herself – was so paramount.

I didn't much like what was in my head. So I dedicated time, effort, and energy to do things with anyone who appeared to be better than I was.

It's a new world when you lack a context for people; you sense they're with you because they feel obliged, and/or you act as though you're fully recovered. Whether this was escapism, coping mechanism, or not yet a DSM[2]–ism doesn't matter. I needed, desired, and sought time with friends and I tried to move Heaven and Earth to make it happen.

Earlier in my story, I touched on not realizing, remembering, or appreciating that people had plenty of things happening in

---

[2] DSM stands for The Diagnostic and Statistical Manual of Mental Disorders and is published by the American Psychiatric Association.

their lives. That I did not have much going on is an understatement. Of course, I'm not including:

- Three kinds of therapy
- Working out five days a week (two of those with a trainer)
- Trying not to be a complete bitch to my parents
- Hoping to sustain my friendships
- Trying to find a boyfriend (check the next chapter), and
- Making every possible effort not to think about what had happened on February 12th and why it had happened.

These things weren't *real* to me. They were tools and tactics needed to rebuild my life and myself. They had to be done.

Now, I am the first to say that my expectations of others were completely unrealistic. I didn't realize this, and I acted accordingly (more on this to follow). I was afraid to say, "You know, beyond really wanting to see you and catch up, I need to hang with my people and you're one of them. Is that cool?"

I was embarrassed to say this.
I was ashamed to say this.
And, **because I felt scared and ashamed, I acted in ways that really didn't reflect who I was.**

I was self-centered.
I lacked empathy.
I pretty much faked everything.

I thought that if I could fool other people that I was okay, I would teach myself that I was alright. Right? Reverse psychology on myself. There was no teaching here; there was just fooling.

A little bit about Ohio and me:

- I was born in New York City.
- When my father was offered a terrific job in Cleveland, he, my mother, and I moved there. (I was 18 months old when this happened.)
- My brother was born there, and we grew up in one of Cleveland's suburbs.
- I went to Barnard College, which supported my life-long plan to live in New York.
- I returned to Cleveland to attend law school at Case Western Reserve University, graduated in 1999, and returned to New York to work in December of that year.
- Two of my closest friends attended law school with me; they live in Cleveland with their families.
- A few friends from high school live in Ohio.
- A few of my parents' friends (some of whose children had gone to school with my brother and me) were poised to become my friends.

So, I have history in Ohio, and was set up for success in many ways when I learned I'd be living there for several months.

What Ohio could offer – being familiar, comfortable, and affordable – was not lost on me. And it made for some challenges.

There isn't much, if any, single shaming in New York City. That's not the case all over the US, and it's certainly not this way in Northeast Ohio. Besides the awkward pauses when you answer questions like, "Are you married?" "Do you have children?" "Is your husband with you?" and the uncomfortable moments when someone who hasn't seen you in years and never heard that you'd broken up with your fiancé more than five years ago states somewhat loudly, "I heard you got married!" (to which I quietly replied, "I'm sorry, you must have confused me with someone else."), the ranks tend to be closed. Because to be 34-35 and *not* be married is not anathema, it is unexpected. And, that person has to be different.

The geography, community, and space were as safe and supportive as one could hope. It just wasn't my home. I know now that I worked against any real progress and any true steps towards feeling happy by acting how I did when spending time with established friends and new friends. Want to hear about some of these?

Because I needed more than ever to have things to look forward to, I stacked my schedule with as many social events as I could make happen. The first of these, a day and a half after arriving in Ohio, was coffee and ice cream with friends I had not seen since law school graduation (May, 1999) and I encouraged them to bring their children. They had married several years prior and happened to live near our law school. Whatever I thought our relationship was, and the specifics elude me now, I behaved as though we were super close. I had presents for the kids, whom I had never met, and I had little to no context for what this couple had been doing. That afternoon, I acted eager (which surely came off as odd), bouncy (which likely was seen as agro and anxious), and loquacious (which surprised no one, I'm sure). I have not seen them since that afternoon.

I know now that the fuel powering me then was a combination of **relief, gratitude, and fear**.

Relief, gratitude, and fear share three attributes: **malleability, intensity, and the potential to be misused and misapplied**.

Less than a week later, someone who had been a friend in law school invited me to join him and his wife, whom I had yet to meet, for dinner and a concert. Not only was I psyched to see my friend and meet his wife, the performing artists were two singer-actors I had loved since I was nine years old (Patty LuPone and Mandy Patinkin, if you were curious). I wasn't allowed to drive so they picked me up and we went to dinner.

At dinner, I know that I amped what I naturally do. I always ask servers what their names are (which I did that evening), I think I tried to show how smart I was about the menu, and I'm pretty sure I flirted with the waiter. And I asked questions. That's what I do. I don't tend to reveal much about me unless you ask questions or want my perspective.

Kate fueled by adrenaline, appreciation, and desperation is not a Kate you want to hang with if you haven't hung with the real Kate in some time. Because a lot is already enough. When you can't lower her volume, it's a whole other story.

I didn't realize that it might have made the experience more enjoyable and comfortable, not just for them but for me, had I voluntarily shared a few things about my previous months. During the meal, I sensed that we had little to nothing in common. I don't practice law. I have nothing to do with the court and incarceration systems. I'm not politically conservative. I wasn't (and I'm still not) married.

Everything I experienced – and presented! – during my first few weeks outside of the hospital was in IMAX.

That night the lack of alignment between us was made really clear when they wanted to leave during the intermission. I agreed to this and claimed not to like the concert anyway. What else could I do? Stay in his seats (which were comped, he told me) and get a car to my parents' house? (Uber did not yet exist.)

During the ride to my parents', I felt for the first time in a while what the feeling of obligation can do. The conversation was stilted, and I could tell my friend was annoyed to drive 45 minutes out of his way, only to then drive himself and his wife home. While "Let's get together again soon" or something resembling it was said, I knew it wasn't meant.

I thought, and I still think, that they asked me to go to the show because I had sent them a wedding gift even though I couldn't attend the wedding (I was still in the hospital and even if I had been released, airplane travel was out of the question for a few months). Yes, I had given them a wedding present. That's what I do for friends. We saw each other one time since that night. I went to their house for dinner when I could drive.

Like all living things, friendships evolve.

We can't force people to accept us and like us.
We can't pretend to be someone else or quiet who we are. (Well, we can do that, and nothing good ever comes of it.)
And we can't hate ourselves when we just don't feel connected to someone anymore.

Just as we can't pretend to be another person because we think it will make us likable, we need to trust our instincts when our interaction with someone who may have once been a friend is off. This was the case when my path crossed those I knew during high school. Back then some were friends, some were not. Whoever we once were, the ship had sailed. I told myself, I believed (and I still do) that time with people is a gift.

My new normal was feeling that *I got to* meet people, get to know them, reconnect if necessary, and be friends. This continued for the next few years. "Getting to" wasn't my right; it was a gift.

Everything felt like a gift.

Waking up and seeing the sunrise.
Hearing the buzzer at Quicken Loans Arena when a Cavs game ended.
Seeing my bald head in the mirror and trying not call myself Telly Savalas.
Spending time with people.

Because I attached so much value to being around others, I tried really hard to present myself as all kinds of awesome. I tried too hard, and that was a repellent. The obligatory invitations didn't come that much during summer 2009. The ones that did were fairly unpleasant. I did reconnect with friends and make a few new friends. I began to believe that **nothing happens randomly; it's all synchronous**. While geography and life's activities distance us, we are friends and we pick up where we left off when we see each other.

I now know one of friendship's truest gifts: continuous connection that sustains regardless of time, tasks, and thrills.

6

DATING: WHEN YOU'RE READY AND WHAT READY ACTUALLY IS

React:
There is nothing like affection from men who barely know me. Every relationship starts somewhere, with something, and between two somebodies.
Act:
I "get to" do, be, and feel. With very little to do, one of the best things I can do for my happiness and healing is to go out with guys.
Fact:
The path to feeling worthy begins: time with a guy is not the same as, and is in no way a replacement for, time with the right guy.

I began "for real" dating later than most, if not all, of my friends. My first serious boyfriend was responsible for a few significant things, including my early "education" about relationships. After nearly six years together, I still had plenty to learn. It is not an accident that I had not dated much between breaking up with him and when I was hurt. By this I mean that my learning about romantic relationships picked up with a fervor during the spring and summer of 2009. That continued probably until mid- to late 2014.

I was, and am, still learning. Because **when we stop learning, we stop living.**

You've read how I attached great value to feeling as though people wanted to hang with me. People being demonstrative has always been important to me. It became almost *imperative* when I was recovering. Why? After my release from the hospital – and frankly through the next few years – I felt empty.

I felt incapable.

I felt unworthy.

It didn't matter how much I prayed, how many positive affirmations I read and said, and whatever progress I was purportedly making in recovery.

I was still a mess.

I had grown to believe that the actions of and attention from other people were tools to help me rebuild, not only who I once was, who I really wanted to be. Nowhere was this belief better illustrated than by my dating life until sometime in 2014 and how things played out with jobs (more on that later).

I knew a lot of people in Ohio, but the only single males I knew were the sons of friends. So how do you meet future dates and boyfriends? Like almost everything else in life, you go online. My brother Ted recommended that I create a profile on OkCupid. I was unfamiliar with this one, though I had dabbled with LavaLife for five minutes in the three month pause my ex and I took in 2006, and there was a brief stint with eHarmony in 2008 (which I resuscitated in spring

2009). I was essentially starting from scratch. It felt good to post pictures of myself (though I was bald) and candidly share who I was, and who and what I sought (or so I believed at the time).

False confidence was generated when men who appeared to be truly interested in me initiated conversation or responded to my comms. Attention that seemed true, and not shady, became something of a narcotic for me. I'm not proud of that.

My first scheduled date was canceled by the guy, and my first real date was the following week. He kindly met me near my parents' house (I still couldn't drive) and I likely read more into that gesture than he intended. "It's so nice of him to drive out of his way," I told myself and I wondered, "Who does that?"

New Yorkers could write a book about walking the fine line between cynicism and fatalism; if you live in New York City long enough, you'll become a cynic. My inherent cynicism, coupled with my immeasurable insecurity, flavored much of what I thought and felt about relationships for several years. This guy and I scheduled another date for the following week. I invited him to come to my parents' house, I would make dinner, and we'd dine on the patio.

What? Really?

I can't remember if I asked my parents if this would be alright. While that's something I would normally do (ask my parents if I can invite someone to their house), I had not full stepped into who I hoped to be and who I since have become. (Mom and Dad, if I didn't ask, I'm sorry.)

You'd have thought that I was hosting celebrities with all the trouble I went to. I spent hours combing through recipes, looking for the best produce, and everything organic, fair trade, vegan, Paleo, and gluten free. While I love to cook, especially for friends and family, I told myself that I was going to so much trouble to let this guy know how important he was and how much I cared. That was a lie, but I didn't realize that then; it felt comfortable and right. Why did I bust my ass making a special meal for someone I barely knew?

To show him that I was worth spending time with?
To prove that I was not a mess, that I had things together? I *was* put together.
To mask that I was recovering from an injury that could have killed me?

I saw this guy twice again, once on my birthday and once for a concert (Maxwell, in case you're wondering). We have no contact now. That is the case with every man with whom I saw a movie or had coffee, dinner, or a talk that summer, including the man who became my boyfriend.

Is that sad or disappointing? Neither. Each of us has gone on to be who we were becoming, or better. Each of them could be (or is) with their ideal partner.

I can say that now.

During the summer and the subsequent months, I felt devastated when interactions with men led nowhere, including to friendship. That's not an exaggeration.

Why did I feel devastated?

A guy didn't want to spend time with me or talk with me?
A guy didn't find me physically attractive?

A guy only been killing time with me because it was the summer and that's what we do then?

Someone not seeking or wanting time with me confirmed that I was not worth spending time with.

I realize now that I lowered my standards considerably for anyone who appeared interested in knowing me. Nothing winds you up to be a magnet for one-sided relationships quite like that. It's nothing against any guy I met or dated that summer; everyone needs something and someone specific to suit who they are.

I had no business dating during that time. Why was this?

I did not have the foggiest idea who I was, so knowing who I wanted to be with was impossible.

Among the things I did learn that summer was that I prefer to date one person. While this likely was born of my need to focus completely and exclusively on every single thing I was doing, I know now that it's how I am wired. What's now called "casual dating" is something that encourages, and sometimes requires, people to juggle those they are (possibly romantically) socializing with. As someone who thinks that multitasking is a joke, and struggled to the high heavens to do one thing really well in the midst of life's noise and multisensory distractions, I looked for a boyfriend at the wrong time.

It was the wrong time because no one could repair, rebuild, and reframe for me.
It was the wrong time because I was figuring out what made me tick, and what could and would make me truly happy.

It was the wrong time because I needed to be about me, as selfish and odd as that felt, and I denied it.

The man who became my boyfriend that summer lived in Columbus, Ohio and we met on eHarmony. Long story short, it did not take long for us to begin an exclusive relationship. What I am about to share is not intended to reflect poorly on him; these are things that I neglected to recognize as signals that we were not suited.

I denied them.

Why did I deny this evidence? I assured myself all was well by asking myself questions whose answers I already knew.

Who was I to judge him?
Was I not also filled with a slew of errors and failures and broken components?
Wasn't I one of the luckiest and most blessed people in the world to get to date this guy?

Here is where gratitude, feeling grateful, can work against you. One of the presents given to me in 2009 was a terrific book: God Never Blinks, by Regina Brett. Among the things discussed in this book is how survivors "get to" do things and experience everything in their lives.

"Get to."

The idea of *getting* to do things is, I believe, intended to instill and increase our gratitude for being in and of the world. I read the chapter that discusses this and immediately attached a higher appreciation to everything I experienced and everything that happened around me. I still feel this way. **I just applied it too heavily alongside my feelings**

of unworthiness, emptiness, and mistaking attention for affection.

This guy and I got serious quickly. Whether or not his feelings for me were true or if I was a distraction from a city he never seemed to acclimate to and the stress of unemployment is anyone's guess. He lost his job not long after we started seeing each other and it was a few months before he was offered one he wanted in Austin, Texas.

That he had little to no contact with his father and his brother was, honestly, a concern for me because I don't want to know a world where I don't regularly talk with and see my family. To know me is to know my tribe and how important the family we make for ourselves can be. That he could distance himself with what seemed to be ease ought to have told me how he connects, or does not connect, with people. All I opted to focus on was he cared about me. He wanted to spend time with me. In the nearly 12 months we dated, I met only two of his friends (and their son) while he met several of my friends and my parents, and did not engage in conversation with any of them.

I told myself that he was shyer and more introverted. It never occurred to me that his lack of effort reflected his overall way of being in the world. I just figured he was close with the people who were most important to him, including me.

As we walked from a restaurant in Austin to his car, I asked him why he didn't really talk to my friends we'd just had dinner with. He told me that he wanted us to discuss what we have in common (two of us are makeup artists). When I asked why he didn't talk about what he does for work, what he knows about life in Texas, or got to know my friends who live in Texas, he was short with me and let me know that he wasn't interested in knowing my friends.

That was the beginning of the end for us.

I had flown to Austin to welcome him belatedly to the city. Because he told me he saw the job there as a long-term one and was looking forward to getting to know Austin, I participated in intro interviews at University of Texas, Austin Communications College for a Master's degree.

I don't remember how it came up, and he told me something as an offside one night that changed everything. He had only accepted the job offer because Austin was closer than Columbus to Menlo Park, California where his dream job was. He didn't intend to live in Austin any longer than necessary; his goal was Menlo Park. He never told me this until that night. I'm pretty sure he planned never to tell me.

Why was this the tipping point for me knowing that he and I were better off apart?

Besides looking seriously at one of the two-year degrees at UT Austin, I had contacted an appraiser for my apartment and had begun looking for a realtor. I was thinking about leaving my home to live where my boyfriend lived, and was taking the necessary steps to begin this process. Had I done all of that and moved to Austin, only to watch him move to Menlo Park, whether or not we broke up, I would have uprooted myself for the wrong reasons.

These reasons – being with someone is better than being without someone, I like Austin – and the operation of my selective memory – I moved to St. Louis to be closer to my ex and that was the beginning of the end of us – were powerful enough to prompt me to want to move.

I didn't move to Austin. I broke up with him a few weeks later.

A large box was delivered on my birthday without a sender's address, but I saw the postmark was from Austin. I gingerly opened this box to see a handwritten note detailing how bad a person I was. The contents of this box were every single thing I had ever given this guy (including half empty bottles of shower gel and books) What was excluded was a very dope button up I'd bought for him at Hugo Boss. The box also contained what looked like two framed pictures that were now pieces of synthetic wood, torn up photographs, and large, sharp pieces of broken glass.

I had a good time bundling all of that up in two tripled bagged garbage bags (except the mean note, which was placed in my Box o' Crap that houses things from which I hope to learn) and hauling them to the basement and the dumpster. Well, maybe "good" is an exaggeration; I was relieved to get rid of those things.

There was still a lot for me to learn about dating and relationships, which continued for the next few years (and will, I am sure, forever). I picked up a few important points during this time:

Where friends (and partners) are concerned, at the very least they need to include you.
They owe you that.
They owe you that not because you earned it, you deserve it, or you're special.

They owe you that because you're you. You're in their lives, and that's how people treat each other, especially people who are close.

When it comes to romantic relationships, **"ready" is knowing who you are, who and what you need, and who and what you want.**

7

FROM OFF THE GRID TO ON THE GRID: RECOVERY IN THE "REAL" WORLD

React:
I don't know what to do. Absolutely no idea. Something is always better than nothing.
Act:
Do things. Do lots of things. Especially anything that seems to differentiate and distance yourself from your feelings, your beliefs, and your truth.
Fact:
Turn off the stopwatch. Trust that when you're truly ready, you will know what is best.

Whenever some kind of change is pending, we have a choice. We can prepare for it and hope, trust, and believe that things will go in our favor. Or we can dread it, fear it, and resist it. Because when things have been wonky and tough of late, why would this be any different?

Can you guess how I approached my return to New York City?

Today we hear often about "being present," and how important it is to be in and of where we are, what we're doing, and who we are. Being present is the modern way of saying "focused," "not distracted," and "completely involved." **It's easy to be present when want to be where you are, are doing what you want, and are happy with who you are. But, when you don't care, or when you hate what's currently happening, you will go elsewhere.**

I had dreamt for months about my return to New York City, and I romanticized it. While I didn't have a job there, and I had not seen the majority of my friends in months, it still felt like my home. On September 5th, when my father and I drove to New York, the script was going to be flipped.

Or so I thought.

I wasn't ready to step back into "regular" life.

It's not as though I had fallen into a Real Housewife routine of lunches, blowouts, and shopping. I had few distractions, commitments, and activities other than therapy, personal training, and seeing family and friends.

My head was filled with a lot of nonsense. While I knew (via a journal entry I wrote on September 21st) that I needed to review, accept, and start fresh, I did very little of that. What I did was unhealthy and damaging: I compared myself and everything happening to how things once were instead of seeing them for what they really were.

Theodore Roosevelt once said, "Comparison is the thief of joy." There are no truer words.

I had a lot of stuff after spending four months and two weeks in Ohio. Out of the goodness of his heart, my father drove me to New York about eight hours, mostly on I-80, with very little to see out the window. Your mind can do plenty in those hours, especially if it's not operating in particularly positive ways. I forgot that, while coming along the same route in April, I had told myself a series untrue stories. I pressed rewind on an old and really bad cassette, and let it play.

I didn't realize that it was a bad idea to invite my then boyfriend to visit for a week when I had been home for less than two days, but that's what I did. I made my first week home as artificial and escapist (other than paying bills and going to the hospital for my Neuro Rehab evaluation) as possible.

Because that's real, right?
You're here, you're owed some fun, and there's no time like now.
Right?

Nope.

By returning to New York and behaving as though I was a guest and not a resident – both in the city and my own life – **I kept myself off the grid even though my geography had changed.**

Shock and awe, or whatever you want to call how you respond to radically different experiences, is an effective way to bring about change. And New York City shocked and awed me.

The awes consisted of the combination of architecture, art, music, people, and constant opportunities to combine the new and the old or, as I like to say, the current and the classic.

Shocks included how much had changed in less than four and a half months in terms of city life and people's existence, experiences, and behaviors. The burst of the housing bubble in 2008 began New York City's move to a much more commercial place and this was in good effect by the fall of 2009. And people – *my* people – had married, moved, changed jobs, had children, and many other things had happened and were in the process of their lives.

While I did not consider myself to be a self-involved person, I was pretty much all about me for the months in Ohio. I forgot that my friends' lives were not like my life which was, for all intents and purposes, a needle on a stuck record. Fairly soon after returning to New York, seeds of resentment, ambiguity, and self-hatred planted in me. These seeds took root fairly quickly and colored much of what I did and everything I felt for the next several months.

Why?

When you're scared and uncertain, the fastest and easiest concepts to cling to are the loudest and most obvious. **When fear is the fuel, our ego can crush our spirit and heart.** In various ways, I cried out for help without actually asking for help. These included:

- I applied for Neuro Rehab treatment at the hospital where I had been an in-patient for a month and a half because I needed structure and predictability.
- I went to lectures and programs, attended webinars, and bought books with titles like *Why You Can't Find a Job* and *You're Perfect Just as You Are* because I did not have any answers and I figured that other people did. (I was partially correct; had I known what

questions to ask, I could have saved a lot of time and money.)

- Because I doubted what I thought I was geared to do for work, I paid for three runs of aptitude testing, where I learned very little I didn't already know.
- I sought happiness on the surface by shopping for and wearing clothes that were four sizes smaller than what I currently wear, because being thinner felt like a huge accomplishment.
- I accepted the offer to be on the alumnae board of my high school, because having something to do for a place I believed in seemed to make up for not having a place to go every weekday for work.

I learned that **when you don't know how to look for what will make you truly (and long term) happy, you take joys where you find them.**

I learned that when no one has higher expectations for you than you do, you have to know when to say stop, look, and listen.
Counterintuitive? Perhaps.

Still, you won't learn anything new when you're running around in the noise.

Now I know that I didn't have to rush and race because I didn't have an expiration date.

Things don't happen on time; they happen in time.
(Copyright pending.)

8

THE JOB THING: LOOKING FOR ONE AND NEEDING ONE

React:
You're home, you're ready, and you *get to* go back to work. It's time to prove that you're supposed to be here; you owe it to everyone.
Act:
Fueled by how grateful you are to be in and of the world, you hustle hard.
Fact:
Just as you *get* to be where you work, the people you report to and the people you're helping *get to* experience you.

Emily, a good friend and the mother of one of my best friends, is an exceptional woman. Emily says, "People who have nothing to do are really busy."

That is the truth. Emily created the statement about people who duck responsibility for things and are unreliable. While that's not fully applicable to me, I know what it is to not have a job and still want and need to do things.

Why do people work, have jobs, and/or go to the office?

- To make money.

- To become famous.
- To justify what college and/or grad school cost.
- To make sense of what one did in college and/or grad school.
- To contribute to the world.
- To create something.
- To learn.
- To be with people.
- To live in one's purpose.

And I'll go one better:

- To believe and feel that you're in this world for reasons: reasons other than surviving a traumatic experience.

When I returned to New York and tried to find my flow, I realized how much I needed a schedule. Having things to do, appointments, and deadlines was how I usually filled my days. Not having those experiences (and expectations), activities, memories, learnings, and results put me in a constant fog.

Finding a job when I returned to New York was difficult. I picked up consulting projects here and there, none of which were particularly interesting and none of them paid what I later learned (or realized) I was worth.

You may wonder, "If you didn't like the work and the money was crap, why did you take the gigs?" That's an excellent question.

I accepted those assignments because the fuel I was operating on in late 2009 and almost through 2010 was wrong. My fuel was luck, masquerading as gratitude, relief, and what I now call the **MBTYN:** the **Misbegotten Belief That You're Needed.**

The joy, relief, and confidence one can find when he or she feels needed can be dangerous. This feeling can become something of a narcotic, leading to a very unhealthy mode of needing to be needed. This means that a person doesn't feel whole or accomplished without the opportunity to help others.

Let me be clear: **believing that you're needed is not the same as actually being needed.**

This begs the question, why does one *need* to feel needed?

- Is something missing from one's spirit?
- Does the person lack a sense of purpose?
- Isn't it enough to help a person or an organization because there is a need and someone is interested, capable, and dedicated?

Speaking only for myself, there is also the need to find **proof**.

Proof that you're in the world for reasons other than taking up space.
Proof that you can contribute to and succeed in the world.
Proof that it wasn't an accident or dumb luck that you survived something that could have killed you.

In the deepest parts of me, I still could not believe that I was alive. The appreciation I felt for the smallest of things was amped by my knowing that every single thing experienced – the aggressively shill sound of car horns, the line around the corner for a new restaurant, the eight shades of purple in a sunrise sky – was my gift to experience.

It wasn't my right; it was a gift.

And all I did to earn these gifts was wake up from a coma.

I *got to* survive.

I believed that I had done anything to achieve my survival. Were it not for the doctors, nurses, radiologists, EMS, family, friends, colleagues, and angels, I wouldn't have made it. So if I was going to be in the world, there should be reasons besides a crack medical team, prayers, and love.

This is a lot of pressure to put on one's self. Of course, I didn't realize that at the time.

The saying "making up for lost time" never meant anything to me until the fall of 2009 when I stepped back into my life in New York. Of course, I wasn't stepping back into my life; I needed to recreate it, or at least refresh it. So feeling immeasurably grateful to be alive, I ran around and did things.

Did I accomplish much? Not really.

I may have looked, on paper, like I was making things happen. As good as it felt to be busy, I was masking my gargantuan fear that I was not really able to do or worthy of doing what I wanted to do.

If you talk with any musicians, DJs, actors, entrepreneurs, and non-profit leaders who knew me after the accident, I am fairly certain they will tell you that I continuously offered to help them. They never responded with an acceptance (with a couple of exceptions, which I will discuss in a later chapter) and the usual response was: "Thanks. I'm good." I thought people were flattered or overwhelmed by someone offering to help without a self-serving agenda, and I thought they were unsure that I really meant, so I kept offering.

No one thought to tell me, "I appreciate you offering to [do whatever I may need or told you I needed or you intuit or observe that I need]" and:

- "I already have someone who does this," or
- "I am not ready to tackle it," or
- "I don't think I need to do that," or the thing I dreaded most (though it might have helped me to hear it):
- "I don't think you're the right person for this particular task."

For months this felt like shoveling sand into a bottomless hole; it could never be filled. That was me. Over and over. Hustling hard. Going in circles. I have since learned that when you need something, you only have to do two simple things to make it happen:

- **Allow** yourself to let others know that you lack something, you're confused, and you want them to be involved. You need their help. They won't know unless you tell them.
- **Ask** whoever has the means and resources to help you. Remember that the answer we do not have will follow the question we need to ask (copyright pending).

When we do these, there's only one result:

Accomplish.

Remember that you are as capable, talented, and worthy as anyone – including your former self! – to do what and to be where you need and want to be.

9

THE JOB THING: "GETTING TO" CAN PRECLUDE GETTING *ONE*

React:
Everyone's telling me to do things in a particular way. Do what I did before I was hurt. Follow what's familiar. Safety will lead to success. Right?
Act:
Do what others tell you. Do more of it. Do better. Be as refined as possible because you learned stuff in those months off grid. You're doing this because it's what you know.
Fact:
You have recently conquered and accomplished things in various ways. Remember how you did, acknowledge what you learned, and apply those tactics (and your drive) to the present.

Luck (or Lucky) is a funny thing.

It's a word that's thrown around when what people mean to say is "appreciative," "grateful," "relieved," and/or "happy to know that I am skilled/talented/smart/capable enough to earn an opportunity."

Luck is dangerous. Luck has an expiration date.

There is nothing long term about luck. It happens. End of story. You've got to take advantage of everything luck provides for you. I felt like I'd ended my run with Luck (capitalized on purpose). I survived a near-death injury, two and a half weeks in a coma, multiple surgeries, my family still loved (and tolerated) me, I still had friends, I could drive, I could walk, all but one of my five senses operated (due to the injury I don't have a sense of smell), I dated, and I owned my home.

To ask for, need, and desire more was selfish. To want a job that let me contribute while learning was nervy. If someone saw value in what I could do for their business, far be it for me to be anything other than appreciative. I needed to hop to it, get it done, and be sure to get it done so well that they'd be crazy not to hire me again. Each of these professional experiences, including the introductory meetings, was the beginning of a true business opportunity, be it short or long term.

Or so I thought.

It's safe to say that most companies don't hire people for emotional reasons. In job descriptions the list of company desires/necessities is long. There is always an applicant who has all of the attributes, skills, and accomplishments in the job description (because hiring today is an extremely, if not exclusively, literal process).

The hired person knows someone at the company. They're willing to accept a lower salary. They have baseline experience, which makes them trainable. And there are, I am sure, many more reasons.

When I returned home on September 5, 2009, I believed that the tough stuff was behind me and all that would follow was gravy. I happen to exist (for the most part) in the realm of positive psychology. While that serves me, it did not serve me in all the ways it could then because it needed to be powered by truth. By "truth" I mean not only what we want to believe, but also what *actually* is.

What is my stock and trade? In brief, I provide solutions.

When facing something I could not solve – find a job after being off the grid for seven months (almost to the day) – I applied one of the Four Agreements: I asked for help. I asked people I trusted to weigh in. I did most of what they suggested (more on this later). I found ways to contribute at places that would not or could not turn down my offers to help (this is what happens when you work without being paid and you volunteer at not-for-profits). I played the game as I'd played it for the last five years, believing that what once worked would work again. I contacted people I had worked with, reported to, supported, helped, and asked them to refer me to recruiters and keep me in mind if they heard about roles.

I believed to be, and presented myself as, a former agency person, sales and marketing manager, and corporate trainer. I sought jobs doing those things across industries. I remembered how I could adapt to environments and connect with people I had little to nothing in common with other than a shared workplace. I applied for jobs at places and brands I simply loved.

And I did not do this with much forethought.

I neglected to remember that companies prefer to hire what I call low-risk candidates. My application to manage events at one of my favorite restaurants (which has since closed) was likely ignored and sent to the delete file. This also probably happened to my applications for jobs at not-for-profits and academic organizations.

I applied to be a docent at a museum where I'd been a member for several years. The last art history experience I had was in high school, which was not seen as a negative thing. After three interviews, I received the "we don't want you" email. It stated the opposite of what two interviewers had told me. (I took some joy in emailing back to call them out there.)

The son of one of my mother's friends started a journal with his college classmates. She encouraged me to contact them regarding brand development and marketing. I met one of the editors for a drink, drafted and submitted a brand platform, and never heard from them.

I worked with a couple of recruiters who sent me to interviews at small companies and agencies, none of which went well. I came up during a time when interviewers not only let you know they were hiring another candidate, they gave feedback so you would have some insight as to why you weren't successful. Things had changed. Understatement.

I joined organizations geared for people in my former industries. I became a member of groups where my square peg-round hole persona was not only obvious, it made things somewhat unpleasant. I took classes (copy editing, career change, building your own website, CSS/HTML) in an effort to expand my skills and perhaps to find a new career path. I learned that taking classes with millennials when you're 40 requires a completely new perspective, people claim to be "experts" to justify charging people, and consultants can find another revenue stream as instructors, even if they can't teach.

I cast my line wide and far to learning and development, female entrepreneurialism, digital marketing, content development, and messaging. I thought I would find something if I left no stone unturned. I believed I could learn enough to reposition myself if needed. (And who was I kidding? It was needed.)

My skills, my passion for something, and my belief that I could help the business achieve its goals were not sufficient.

Why?!

Honey, it's about money. It's also about how you are perceived and how you appear to be in an organization's culture and ethos. Talent acquisition directors (formerly known as human resource directors) seem to believe that they have psychic powers. They know who they want to work at the company and they will exert their power to reject any applicant that is not a perfect fit. If only job descriptions would include, "If you are not all of this and if you have not done every single thing on this list, save yourself and us some time and do not apply. Thank you and good night."

That's one perspective.

What no one in hiring will tell you is that it's also about you. That you truly, honestly, and without question believe that you are right for the job.

Call it earning. Maybe it's deserving. Perhaps it is your right. Whatever. You know in your spirit, heart, and mind that you are supposed to do that work at this company. When you don't truly feel that way and believe it in your core, you may as well show up to the interview wearing pajamas.

That was me: behaving like someone and not believing in someone. The someone, of course, was me.

I returned to New York with unfamiliar combinations of joy and fear, excitement and dread. While I had done some consulting work for a company in Ohio, it had been months since I had worked in a "real" job. By "real," I mean a position that was enjoyable, in an environment and with a community I liked, and, most importantly, one that I knew I was contributing to in meaningful and measurable ways.

In short, I was desperate to do anything. Where I was in my head and how I felt were dark, empty, hopeless places. I needed to be somewhere that at least appeared to be **better**.

"Better" meaning I did something, helped someone, made a difference, generated sales, and on and on.

"Better" meaning "You heard I died? You thought I was gone forever? I'm back. I'm here. Let's do this."

"Better" meaning doing everything that had nothing to do with who I actually was at the time.

And so it began: my misbegotten efforts to find work, fueled by trust and hope in everyone and everything but myself.

Who I was and *how* I was included being:

- Unprepared for every meeting and call I arranged, other than the interviews at the previously mentioned museum.
- Unaware of how I could show up and contribute in ways that would measurably help the company achieve.

- Unaware people were taking meetings with me out of obligation or to honor a request from a friend/colleague.
- Unaware of (or unwilling to do?) what I truly wanted to do.
- Unaware of how to position, or re-position, myself for a job I truly wanted – because I was not the same person I was before I was hurt. Rather, I didn't feel or believe certain things the ways I had before the accident.

How I operated during my job search was an example of how my gratefulness for being alive worked against me.

While gratitude is always something to feel and demonstrate, there's a time and a place, as with all things. As I researched the companies I felt lucky enough to land meetings with, I learned as much as possible about the founders, the employees, the accomplishments, the deliverables, the goals, and all the details in the ways I had learned to do during law school. **I didn't identify how and why my being there could help them ascend to whatever peak they sought.**

Why the hell not?

I had created and adopted a belief that everything that happened in my life was something I *got* to do. *Everything* happening was almost not mine to experience. That made every single thing a positive experience, even if it wasn't. Remember how I *got to* wake up in the morning and do everything? It wasn't just insecurity prompting me to ask myself questions I'd never asked myself. It was the "getting to."

Actually, I didn't ask questions of myself: I told myself stories that I know now were entirely untrue:

- You're a sales and development person.
- You haven't worked in agency since 2002.
- You only got this meeting because so-and-so owed what's his name a favor, and meeting with you squares everything.
- All you do, rather, all you're *known* for doing, is all that you are.
- Any job you get is a gift…
- …Thus any amount you're paid, whether it reflects your worth or not, is the ribbon, the icing, the "this is all that you get."

During the months of looking for a job, I learned just how much the hiring process had changed.

Getting hired seemed to happen for people who fit every single sought quality like the last perfect piece of a puzzle. An interview I remember well, in February 2010, was with the New York office of a London-based agency claiming to be in an "innovation space." The recruiter told me that the feedback she'd received about me from an interviewer included that I "didn't match their values." Their values? To land clients, make money, and become known as the big swinging dicks of the "innovation space?"

What the interviewer clearly had not told the recruiter (or the recruiter neglected to take up) was they wanted someone young, unexperienced, and with a glossary culled together from reading TechCrunch, BuzzFeed, and every blog about innovation. Or the interviewer knew I wasn't a fit for their community from the start. The generic feedback reinforced my ever-growing feelings of being the square peg trying desperately to fit in round holes.

Do you wonder how I spent the bulk of my time when I wasn't looking for a job?

I volunteered.

It's safe to say that I needed the people I was volunteering for more than they needed me (and I would come to know this as time progressed). I volunteered primarily at a not-for-profit dedicated to the education and creative development of young people where I'd begun tutoring and workshopping in October, 2008. I made volunteering my job, showing up two or three days a week, eventually also working in its for-profit space. Having worked in the cosmetics industry since 2003, I had become known for training sales teams, writing curricula, leave-behind and take-with collateral, video scripts, packaging text, product names, and taglines. The six or seven freelance gigs I landed between late 2009 and through 2010 consisted of doing those things.

No problem, right?

While the work was not particularly challenging intellectually, some of the people I reported were to - how can I say this with respect? - challenging. I wasn't reinventing the wheel; I was polishing the chromes and cleaning the rims (copyright pending). While I had ideas for enhancing the messaging and refining brand voice to increase sales and marketing reach, those were not why I was hired. I was hired because I could do the work well (the people who hired me did so because they had worked with me or heard a positive referral). I could do the work quickly and I was willing to do the work for, let's just say, less than industry-appropriate payment.

What you do for work has as much to do with who you're working for and with as what you're literally, creatively, and strategically doing.

I was so appreciative to have been hired for however long to do whatever was asked that I bore far more ego-driven nonsense than I'd have ever allowed myself to do before I was hurt. And I *got* to write things. I got to contribute in whatever seemingly meaningful ways I could. I got to meet deadlines that were ridiculous in theory and totally insane in execution. I was spoken to as though I was one of their minions. I got to do everything possible to prove to myself, *not* to the people who hired me, that I was capable and useful, that I could show up and claim my place in a world I had been absent from for several months, and that I could do excellent work. My own expectations were so much higher than any of the managers'. I sensed this.

I believed that was so (them having lower expectations than I did) because they felt sorry for me.
I believed they figured that I'd do my best because they'd known my work was good.

While I never inquired if those things were true, I know now that in business, people don't hire because they feel sorry for you. They may hire you because you charge less. And I can't imagine anyone sacrificing high quality deliverables – which they claim as their own work – for lower rates.

The light at the end of the tunnel seemed to arrive in late December 2010 when I landed a job at a company whose product launch I'd written about and trained when it premiered at Sephora. Working for someone I liked and respected, having reported to her at my last company job in a retail environment I knew well about products I believed in were positive components. That's the story I told myself.

Nothing could have been further from the truth.

Things had really changed at Sephora while I was in recovery. I learned, a couple of months after starting there in January 2011, that the person who'd had the job prior to me had not showed up for scheduled meetings and events. When his stores ran low on inventory, he didn't step in to increase distribution. I thought the stores hated me. Why else would they deny my efforts to connect with staff, increase sales, and host events? I thought it was me. What else could it be? On a team conference call one day, the VP said that I was acting as though I worked for Sephora and not for the company and asked if I knew what I was supposed to do. What I wanted to say back to this person, who had hired her son to work on our sales team, was, "Why did you hire me?"

Working for this company in this role was emotionally exhausting. And it required me to play a role I'd never played since I began working in cosmetics: an observer, not a performer. It was as though everyone I worked with on the client side and in-house was speaking Farsi and I only knew Sanskrit. I had participated in the game one can play with herself – self-hatred, aka how much do *you* suck? – for several months and, now I could turn the volume way up: I must suck pretty bad to have decided to take this job and dread every single day.

And, I *got to* deal with this.

It was up to me to leave this opportunity, environment, and culture. In chapter 12 I'll tell you about the experience of leaving this job and starting a business with someone.

Not long ago, I realized how I could have managed the (not to dramatize) nightmare that this job was. I had fixed, overcome, and conquered challenging things earlier in my life. Just like I got to write, train, and be the proverbial whipping boy at this job, **I *got to* step out on faith, trusting that I *could* do because once I *had* done.**

What do I mean?

During the nearly 16 months I figured out what the hell I needed to do to find a meaningful job, **I forgot about the unexpected bends in my life's linear path and how I had handled them.**

My professional life began in a fairly linear way, as things tend to for Gen X'ers: I went to college, graduated, went to graduate school, and got a job. These included not really liking where I'd gone to college, other than matriculating at a college in my birthplace, studying at London School of Economics during my junior year, making friends, and connecting with one administrator, one staff person, and a handful of professors.

How could I have forgotten that going to law school was not my first choice post-college (and when the jobs paid a $19,000 salary in 1996, I knew that the jig was up)? I still can't believe that not passing the Bar Exam in 1999 was an experience that I endured, processed, and flipped. I quit my job (which was one of the happiest company jobs I ever had) to move to St. Louis where my then-boyfriend lived without securing a job there before moving. I did this having trusted someone I worked for who never gave me any real reason to believe that he'd make a call on my behalf to a sister agency.

And when I got to St. Louis, I worked for someone who became, and still is, a very close friend and mentor in a job that was found purely by my efforts and my ways of doing things.

Not one of these, I guess I can call them accomplishments, occurred to me as I sought and struggled to find a real job after seven months off the grid.

Note to self – and to you – **remember the times when you showed up and kicked ass your way.**

You can.

I can.

It happened once or (if you're me, and maybe for you) it happened several times.
It happened with limited insight and fewer resources.
You showed up because you could.
You learned from every single place and environment, every person and culture.
You can apply what you learned to the new whatever-it-is.

When you apply what you've learned, you will do – and you will be! – so much better. You'll do things clearer, stronger, and truer.

Why?

Because you're wired that way.

Because you can.

10

THE PERSONAL, THE SEQUEL: QUICK TO TALK MAKES QUICK TO WALK

React:
Someone no longer cares about me. I don't know this person to be thoughtless, and since when do my calls go unreturned? I am officially confused, hurt, and angry.
Act:
If you don't want to be around me, I'll help you out. As much as your life is different now, mine is too. I'll show you that by acting busy and focused on other things and other people.
Fact:
Before you do anything aggressive, particularly around someone who has been key in your life, do these first: Stop. Process. THEN say and do something, or not. Because once it's done, you are done.

I looked forward to several things upon my return home to New York. One of those was spending time with my close, longtime friends who lived in the boroughs, like my college roommate, a couple of work colleagues, and the friend from college who had been with me the day I was hurt. We had become close friends. While we are no longer friends, I know now I was primarily responsible for the deterioration of our friendship.

This chapter was very difficult to write, and I hope that my sharing what I felt, did, and ultimately learned will help everyone who faces a crisis with a friend. Because friendships with people who have become family are too valuable to lose. We must endeavor to protect, repair, and retrieve.

She and I used to talk, text, and hang out regularly. That stopped after I was hurt (it couldn't happen between me being in two hospitals and then in Ohio). It didn't pick up again once I returned to New York City. Between my fear, confusion, resistance, and whatever was happening on her end, less than a year passed before our friendship terminated.

My friend's birthday was 11 days after I returned home. I called her that day. Things felt different, whether she heard the fear in my voice or she was dealing with being pregnant (which I learned that day) I couldn't identify. I felt distant.

It did not take me long to convince myself that she was living her life, and there was no room for me in it. When I felt really upset, I said that she didn't want me in her life.

Being and behaving in the present is usually a good way to be. **Sometimes we need to call upon how we were in the past to do what's right and what's best in the present.** Unfortunately, that is not how I acted.

There was the old me – before I was hurt – and the *new* me: a survivor and a fairly lost and unsure person. To this day I don't know why I didn't call upon my known behaviors to resuscitate and sustain our friendship. I was probably embarrassed, ashamed, and thought that I was the only one of the two of us who cared. Those, of course, are poor reasons. For someone who I had once thought of as a sister, I owed her, and me, a helluva lot more. Our time together during these months was wonky and infrequent.

This was to be expected with her working, being pregnant, and married. I, on the other hand, stayed busy finding things to do, looking and applying for jobs, and trying to reorient myself to life. When I was sarcastic over email, I did not know she was upset by that until a mutual friend told me a few months later. She and I eventually discussed this over dinner, and I apologized, and it seemed we both really wanted to reconnect. We saw each other only one more time before our friendship ceased. I went to her apartment to see her, her infant daughter, and her parents after a pediatrician appointment. I had never felt so much like a guest. That was because of me, not anything that they said or did.

A week or so later I got a ping that I was tagged in a picture with the baby girl with a series of family and friends. The picture of me was unflattering, and what hurt (silly ego) more than that was the caption on mine was "Kate and (baby's name)" while every other caption was a nickname, an aunt, an uncle, a godparent, a loved one. I was just "Kate." Whether it was my frontal cortex or just me being an insecure bitch, I asked her to untag me from the picture.

Who *does* this?

Someone who is scared. And **when we're scared, the shallowest things about us rise to the surface.**

Fast forward to my calling her and reaching out, never to hear anything. Anyone who knows me well will surely tell you that the way to really mess up my mojo is to not reply to me. Whether you're silent or you're ghosting, I do not respond well to one-sided communications.

I had had it. I felt ignored and rejected. I called her, hoping she would pick up, and when she didn't, I left a voicemail, which was the worst thing to do. I said something resembling, "There's no point in identifying who's at fault because we both know that our friendship has pretty much run its course. You can tell me that you don't believe this by calling me back within a week. If you don't, I'll know that we are done. Hope to hear from you. Take care."

How would you respond to that? You may do what she did – or didn't do – and not return my call. So that was it. We had been friends from 1995 to 2010. Longer than some marriages, shorter than something I thought would be for life. I spoke with my brother shortly after this happened (or didn't happen) and learned that she had Facebook messaged him when her husband had been hurt. I had no idea this happened. It had happened the week (or right around the time) I had commanded her to call me.

What could I do?

Immediately I wondered what it would say about me if I contacted her with concern and apology. Why did she tell my brother and not me? Would she have called me back whether or not her husband was safe and unharmed? So I didn't contact her. I said prayers for her husband's recovery and ones of relief when he was alright. I did not reach out to either of these people who had been important in my life for years just because I was ashamed and scared.

Feeling ashamed. Feeling scared. Those are terrible reasons not to do something you know is right.

That's not the only thing I did wrong, or didn't do, in 2009-2010. I did not contribute in any real way to restoring a friendship that had once been crucial to me. All the things I knew to do, all the ways I knew to be, were chucked to the wayside.

I could have approached our reconnect as though it was our friendship before I was hurt. It didn't occur to me to do that. I was different, she was different, and significant things had happened in both of our lives.

So what?

Relationships evolve, sometimes by choice and sometimes by necessity. When you care about the person, it's possible to focus on what they mean to you. Or, your ego can get in the way and you can spend time thinking about what's different and what isn't happening, laying blame, and being confused.

If she reads this book, which is unlikely, I hope she will get to the next passage. For readers, for people who know me, for her, and for myself, what follows is something of an accountability list. This list includes things I wanted to do, things I didn't know how to do, things I promised to do eventually, and things I now know are imperative.

- I didn't pepper you with calls and texts like I always had before things changed.
- I didn't research what those in the company of trauma survivors can go through.
- I didn't research what it's like to be pregnant.
- I didn't offer to help (except once, if memory serves) and let you know that I was there for you.
- I had the gall to make the only picture that will ever exist of your older daughter and me about me and my self-hatred.

- I made personal whatever you said and did, and didn't say and didn't do.
- I didn't search for your address and send you my letter to make amends; I only called you and emailed it.
- I didn't ask you if I had said or did anything to upset you because I was too scared and ashamed.
- I'm pretty sure I never thanked you for all you and your husband did in the immediate aftermath of my being hurt; I apologize from the bottom of my heart.

All of this to say, **I wasn't empathic. I believed that trauma and post-trauma were exclusive to me.** You had been through, and were *going* through, so much. All I thought about was my own stuff. I have no one to blame for the end of our friendship but myself. I did it.

I don't have the science on this, but I believe that **fear is a fuel that accelerates and adjusts what we do**.

When you're upset, or angry, you want to deal with it immediately. The filter evaporates, the volume is amped, and 99% of the time, there is nothing to be upset about. We feel it when something has been affected by fear. And like brownie batter made with rotten eggs, we've got a straight up wrong product. All of these feelings are deep-seeded pains and feelings:

Hurt.
Ignored.
Abandoned.
Judged.
Unloved.

If you're a trauma survivor, you're a little more inclined to feel these. You can concoct darkness from basic, alkaline statements and behaviors. So what the hell can we do about it?

Stop.

- Breathe.
- Be still.

Process.

- Did you hear what was *actually* said, or have you attached a context and a framework that were not intended?
- Ask yourself if your history with the involved person gives good reason to think they acted unkindly to you.

Say something *before* you do anything.

- Check your fear, insecurity, and self-doubt; remove them from your mind.
- Seek clarity. Trust me, you need it.
- The only answer we don't have is from the question we did not ask. Nowhere is this truer than in the realm of personal relationships.

Is this a lot to ask when you're this close to yelling though a bullhorn to people who lean on their horns in rush hour traffic? Yes.

That's too bad. You need to do this.

Your relationship is worth that, because your friend is worth it, and, most importantly, **you are worth it.**

11

GHOSTS: HOW TO MANAGE THEM

React:
Ghosts. How and why did it go from spending this wonderful time with someone and then they're suddenly gone? No explanation, no reason given. It must be that I am a disaster and repellent to people.
Act:
Spend loads of time trying to figure out what you did to make someone not want to know you. Try to find them. Hate yourself during this process.
Fact:
Ghosts. There is no solution. People will do what they want. Relationships have expiration dates and they can be controlled by one party, not both. You choose to be in it, they choose not to be in it. Accept and release.

This chapter follows on purpose the conversation about a relationship's destruction. It is like the other side of the coin to that story. Whether it is or not, it is something I learned more recently and it feels right to include it here.

"Why does it hurt so bad?"

This is the title of a song by Whitney Houston (RIP) on the soundtrack of "Waiting to Exhale." It's a song that has always resonated with me. I ask this question over and over again. I don't know why it bothers me so much when people go ghost. This was not an issue for me before I was hurt.

You've likely identified that I am very interested in why things happen and how I can identify, investigate, understand, resolve, and hopefully get to an accepting, sense-making place. Before I was hurt, this stuff didn't bother me:

> You don't want to be friends?
> Fine.
>
> Not interested in working together or collaborating?
> No shine off my sun.
>
> You're not someone who returns calls or replies to emails?
> You're annoying and you lack good manners and I just do not care.

As recently as early 2017, I shed tears over a man I was becoming friends with who went ghost. I cried because out of nowhere, it was, "See ya. We're done." Not that he said anything; he just disappeared.

One-sided relationships are the bane of my existence. Truth.

Why I am so sensitive to this is somewhat odd. It's not a fear of abandonment. It isn't the dread of living alone for the rest of my life. I spent a great deal of time by myself, literally and figuratively, without much say in the matter. There isn't anything that hurts me more than a relationship stopping without knowing why.

It's a holdover from feeling that all the things in my life I *get to* experience. And I came very close to experiencing nothing and no one in mid-February 2009.

That's my truth.

I have had time to think, talk, and ruminate about this. I have *made* time to do things with professionals, friends, and people I admire. Here is what I know now:

It's not you; it's life.

People have loads going on that you're not aware of.

They marry, move, change jobs, become pregnant, and tons of other happenings that have nothing to do with you. It doesn't feel like that, though, because there was a time when you shared all of your nonsense and all of your important stuff with each other. They had you on speed dial, text, Facebook, and all means of communication.

Maybe they developed interests you don't share.
Maybe they thought you have a lot going on.
Maybe you grew apart.

Maybe someone realized that what you had in common, what held you together was not glue; it was taffy and it dried out. Of course, it would be awesome – and kind, respectful, loving – if someone could tell you, "I appreciate our friendship, but it is finished." That just does not happen.

It would be even more awesome if you said or did something hurtful to a friend without realizing it and they told you right then and there, "What the hell?! Slow your roll." And if they don't happen to tell you immediately, they call you out when the dust settles. You then have the opportunity to clarify, course correct, and be accountable for hurting them.

They are worth that. You are worth that.

We can't count on those things happening. That's one of the reasons **we must think before we speak** (or email or text). Remember that perception won't always play well with intention. Relationships – good, healthy ones – are composed and conducted by *all* parties involved. They are not solo acts. When someone – maturely or not – lets you know that they are done, which means that you are done, walk away. Be brave.

Trust and believe that you are worth more. Trust and believe that you will find people who are aligned with you in being demonstrative and communicative.

Trust and believe that they are searching for you, just like you are searching for them.

12

WORKING: A JOB WHERE THE PUZZLE PIECES DON'T FIT

React:
Anything is better than this. Friends will work well together.
Act:
Learn as you go, money solves problems, and stopping what you're doing is a sign of weakness. Don't ask questions. Don't seek clarity. You're already annoying enough to people. You started this and you will finish it on your terms.
Fact:
Not knowing prevents you from doing things in the best possible ways. As uncomfortable as it may be to ask "What? Why? How?" you must ask. It is dark when we are unaware; truth brings light.

In January 2011, I began the first full-time company job I had since February 2009. I was excited. Understatement. Earlier in the book, I touched on its challenges and that I eventually quit. There isn't much to share about this five and a half month experience, other than what follows here.

Nothing about this job was enjoyable, intellectually challenging, or stable. And I was grateful to have it. If the brand didn't sell $10M that year, its primary retailer was going to drop it. There were 44 stores in my territory. The company owned three brands I was responsible for, didn't market to audiences, and didn't update their websites. I still told myself every day that I *got to* have this job. By late February, I knew I wanted to quit. I had never felt so lonely and disconnected. The challenge with the job may have been affected by a new relationship with a guy that that seemed to be going well which ended in March.

I was in a bad place (two years from being hurt) and the job wasn't helping. In the second chapter of Regina Brett's God Never Blinks, the lesson is "When in doubt, just take the next right step," which varies based on what you're doing. For me, the next right step was to leave this job. **When you're unhappy, anything other than what you're currently experiencing appears to be better.**

By the early spring, I was in a particularly vulnerable place, fairly uncertain about everything, and eager to get gone from the job. One night around this time, a colleague/friend suggested that we start a business together – a makeup studio.

May 21st was my last day at the job. Immediately, my soon to be business partner and I kicked into high gear: contract, Chamber of Commerce, interior design, supplies, inventory, logo, signage, insurance, income, brand, marketing. The business was going to be in New Jersey, a couple of minutes from her house. You may wonder why my previous list does not include things like budget, responsibilities, and goals. And, other than identifying that we'd be based in New Jersey and do offsite work in New York and Connecticut, that I was back of house (marketing, communications), she was front of house (artistry, media, sales), and that I'd come to the site two or three times a week, we did not hash out really important things.

Those included:

- Estimated unexpected costs (other than rent and monthly overheads)
- Side hustles
- Schedules
- Each of our commitments outside of the business (read: expected availability)
- Thorough review of our contract by a third party (read: someone who had not drafted the agreement)

Let me be clear: my friend and (now former) business partner did not do anything wrong. Her plans and goals were hers, her way of doing things was hers, and she invited me to be in her life and eventually facilitate what she was doing. I did not ask certain questions. I was very caught up in the environment and experience and how they were radically different to where I had been earlier in 2011. I neglected to demand that an attorney review the agreement before we signed it. Someone at LegalZoom drafted the material and it was likely a rote document. I say this because it lacked a buy-sell agreement. A buy-sell legally binds a business's co-owners if one chooses to leave, is forced to leave, or dies. In brief, when one partner departs, someone can buy their share of the business; what events can trigger the buyout, and how much the departing partner will be paid for their interest in the partnership. Buy-sell agreements protect co-owners.

I paid for the majority of our startup costs, including insurance, flooring, furniture, half of the saleable inventory, supplies, and the website design and monthly hosting, I bought my partner an iPod for accepting credit card payments with Square, and I opened a checking account with my own money. We agreed to take turns paying the rent and I covered the month she could not pay. I sensed that costs could be an issue from the start and I brushed it under the rug because it had always been my goal to have my own business that turned a profit.

I chose to dedicate 100% to the business. My partner took work at a beauty counter in the nearby department store. I didn't ask about her availability until it occurred to me that if she was scheduled at the department store, she was not available for our clients. I did not ask her if a portion of her earnings would go back into the business. I did not know how to ask the question without appearing bossy or greedy. I forgot that we were fifty-fifty partners.

She had told me in late March, when we had a reconnect dinner before the topic of business was raised, that she and her husband had two children, the younger of whom was diagnosed with a serious illness. Once we were in actual talks about going into business, I did not ask her if her child's care would have a significant impact on her schedule. I neglected to ask about expenses and the necessary income to manage those. I still don't know why we didn't discuss these things.

Part of me thinks it didn't occur to me; part of me knows I felt cruel and inhuman to ask. A few things happened that called into question whether she and I were on the same page. All of these had to do with expectations, clarity (or lack thereof), money, and time.

I know that from start to finish, we both did our best.

I realized in the fall of 2011 that she was better suited to run the business by herself. Truth be told, I am also a solo flyer. I had begun to believe that I was only sought because I could provide money, not my marketing skills, brand development experience, and ability to write. I was still raw, vulnerable, and scared when she approached me about starting the business. Earlier that year I had accepted a job in an organization with people who, other than a couple of exceptions, were not ideal for who and where I was at this time. It was pretty much a disaster from day one.

And I was carrying all of that when we initially discussed, and eventually decided, to start the business.

I don't believe in coincidences. I believe in synchronicity. She proposed the business at a time when I needed to do something else, so I accepted her offer. Being completely honest, I did not think about it with the depth of which I was capable.

Why not?

I thought that starting and running a business was *it*. It wasn't a unicorn by any means. Because it came to me via a person I liked and trusted, at a time that was so completely twisted, I felt that I could rescue myself with this.

Little did I know.

I did not take advantage of the opportunity to get answers, and thus clarity, during the partnership.

If you grew up as I did, you learned a couple of things about getting answers. First, you should (a *very* dangerous word) know and it's only from your neglect, idiocy, and ignorance that you don't. Second, asking someone to explain or clarify what they mean when they said or did something indicates your stupidity, foolishness, and/or ignorance. It's amazing how this programming sticks to us like Gorilla Glue on plastic.

I felt ridiculously embarrassed to ask someone to explain what they just did. This time in my life led me to create the phrase, "I'm intuitive, not psychic." It wasn't as though people attended accelerated business school or advanced certification programs while I was off the grid. Everyone, including my business partner, seemed to be informed and trained far more, and far better, than I was.

I told stories to myself. They included how asking my business partner to clarify and keep me in the loop would make her feel judged. She would feel that she had done something wrong. She had enough going on with her family; she didn't need me to challenge her.

It was my right as her business partner to learn what had changed and what was happening. As much as my asking her would be an indication of my trust in and respect for her, I did not want to upset her. It's bad enough to feel stupid. To make someone angry is so much worse. Or so it seemed.

In January 2012, I reached my tipping point. As much as I'd been living powered by gratitude, I had come to truly believe that I was **worthy**.

Worthy of looking forward to each day.
Worthy of feeling appreciated.
Worthy of earning against my investment.

I wanted to have a positive relationship with my business partner. Leaving the business could ruin our friendship. And I knew that we were not meant to be in business together. My friend eventually closed the business and renamed it to reflect what she is doing with a range of makeup artists.

I believe that **people are in our lives to bring us joy, teach us something, or both.** This experience brought me both I continue to learn from the small business community. During 2011-2014, I learned a great deal about expectations (and that we must release them) and how what we resist persists. While I was in this particular business, **I confused proving to myself that I could be successful with proving that to other people.** I focused on the latter. I know now that their evaluation meant nothing.

The fog created by fear and flux can be our undoing when we refuse, resist, or are unable to learn first and then state who we are, what we want, and why we do.

Fact: you can't do things effectively without the necessary knowledge.

For the seemingly endless, yet actually infinitesimal, time it takes us to say, "That's not clear to me, could you circle back and help me understand?" we will get what we need to get things done.

You'll learn. Someone else will learn. Egos be damned.

Soldier up. You deserve to operate in clear skies.

Founding and leaving the makeup studio were steps in my very long journey. This journey, which began back in 1999, had a purpose: to figure out who the heck I was and how I was going to be in the world. The time had come to go outside my known circles of solutions and find new answers.

13

COACHES, GUIDES, TEACHERS: LEARNING FROM THEM AND REFUSING THEM

React:
Many people have recommended someone and talks about them like they are Yoda. I could learn new things, active things, to make me, how I am in business, and my life better.
Act:
Invest time, energy, and money into consults and courses with coaches. Dedicate. Hope. Ultimately feel rejected, disconnected, and disappointed when the results are not what you expected and what was promised. Tailspin.
Fact:
When you pay for coaching and consulting, you are within your rights to expect solutions, solace, whatever was sought and promised. Remember that what you need from others cannot be provided (whether or not they use a templated program or method) when you are not ready or willing to hear them.

I grew up at a time in the US (1980s) where asking for help was something you did not do. You listened. You learned. You tried. You succeeded. Coaches were for sports.

Fast forward to today's personal development industry. There are "coaches" for everything. When you're vulnerable, unsure of what to do, and eager to flip the script you are an ideal client for those who run programs.

And when you're vulnerable, unsure, and mega eager, you're also geared to fall face forward when you participate.

Choosing to leave the makeup business I founded with my colleague was a good idea in theory – it wasn't serving my long-term plans, I wasn't earning money from the business, and it wasn't benefiting me.

And just as I had begun the business without applying ninja-like thought and research, I left it without an organized – or a specifically identified! – destination. This is a key ingredient in the recipe for doing things for the wrong reasons. Of course, I did not realize that at the time.

So what to do?

Other than volunteer at organizations and apply for jobs, I had time. With that time came opportunities to dig deep and make things clearer and better.

How did I dig deep and find clarity? Rather, how did I attempt to do those things?

I became clients for two different consultants and participated in some well-known programs for women's development. Not quite a month before I left the makeup studio, I broke up with a guy I had been seeing for a few months. Single, not entirely by choice, and with a record of relationships appropriate for the standup circuit, I decided I needed a new perspective.

During an event at an organization for women entrepreneurs, I saw a presentation by a woman who coaches on healthy relationships. She struck me as modern, smart, and kind. I looked at her website, spoke with her, and became one of her clients in a six-month program.

The first exercise was a good one: find an image and caption it with how I wanted to feel and what I wanted to happen when I encountered a man I had been seeing. I have that document still, and I feel, as I did in February 2012, as passionately and strongly about what I wrote now as I did then. If only the rest of the program continued in this way. The coach chose to reveal the program's components only at the start of each month. The first meeting was a series of questions about my personal and dating history. The next two months were about my parents' relationship and their relationships with me. Whether I was not ready or willing to do this or it was just not useful, I wasn't having it.

I was 37 years old.
I had been engaged.
I'd had exclusive relationships three or four times.
I knew what my patterns were.
I knew what my triggers were.

Before the third month began, I politely inquired if the program was about what can be learned from my parents' marriage. When she said yes, I told her that I was not the right person for her process, being rooted in family stuff. We were not a fit. She said she would cancel my recurring payment and I was no longer her client.

What I ought to have done here is back up and ask myself why I had sought counsel from a third party. What was really going on with me?

Instead of being Sherlock Holmes on my own self, I jumped feet first into a relationship with a consultant who worked with small businesses on their marketing strategies. I had learned about this person when she was on a learning call with the relationship coach. I was raw from the makeup studio experience. I had been thinking for a while about hanging my own shingle and making my own brand strategy/messaging/marketing services for established and emerging businesses profitable. Once again, **I was eager and anxious. Those are not the same as ready and focused.** So I checked out her website, didn't see any red flags, and became one of her clients.

Now, back to the feet first jumping.

My first "grown-up" job was in the digital group at an advertising agency. I know a little bit about the game. My excitement about and belief in this consulting experience were real. That changed after a short time: some of the content, including a useful Q&A, was written by her yet the majority of it was created by other people, including the marketing audio.

Additionally, I was clear from the beginning why I contacted her: I needed to revise and refresh my brand. I was not interested in creating a new brand. When I spoke to her about this, she ducked and covered, and eventually failed to return my calls and emails. And, that was that.

I saw her on the subway a few months ago. I think she saw me. I stood near her seat on purpose, hoping that she might make eye contact. It didn't happen. By this point, I had made my peace with her (misrepresenting, not being accountable) and I had very nearly forgiven myself.

Why would I need to forgive myself?

For spending time and money on material I could have found myself via research.
For believing that anyone other than me could refine *my* message and purpose.
For expecting someone other than me to have the ability to tell the world what I can offer.

Because I value time more than anything else, I'm not particularly good at waiting. Everything that happens is something I get to experience; taking a pause after "learning opportunities" occur is something I have only recently come to do with ease. At this time in my life, I focused on and measured everything that hadn't gone well and everything I did to mess it up.

I like prime numbers. I believe that three is the most powerful digit. So the third self-development/business growth/ women on fire program *had* to be the most useful of my efforts.

Right?

Well, I wish that was the case. Note that there was some overlap with these three experiences, and I learned that it is possible to take on too many things simultaneously. Timing is a notable thing.

Having it on good authority, as well as a positive experience with the founder's public appearances, I signed up for a half year program designed for women to master their lives in every capacity (personal, professional, body, relationships). I'm a graduate of Barnard College. I am familiar and comfortable with women-only environments. This is a perfect time to reinforce one of my core beliefs: **intention and perception don't always align**.

For five months in 2012, we met as a group for two days each month in New York City. The focus area was different each month. Throughout the program actionable things were taught and demonstrated. These acknowledged and dealt with inner and external conflicts, clearing away hurts and fears, and embracing being a woman in emotional, physical, historical, and philosophical ways.

Then there was the "connecting," competing, and bragging.

Each month, we were broken up into smaller groups and assigned to a woman who had "graduated" from the program. We went to lunch nearby and participated in what I came to feel was forced socialization. I attended each lunch hoping to make new friends and be inspired. Whether it was dumb luck (or lack thereof) or what I believed/perceived (there was a lot to process during these weekends and to require people to dine with strangers fresh out of the room wasn't ideal, because the overwhelm was real), people didn't hold eye contact. For the most part, they weren't interested in talking. Correction: they weren't interested in talking with me. During the presentations, people liked to sit with people they knew and the ranks were closed both socially and literally.

Women who know or have learned how to shine will do it exceptionally well, particularly when encouraged. This program provided monthly opportunities for participants to introduce themselves to the world via elevator pitches or questions to a presenter; there were many opportunities for participants to show up and show off. I worked in corporate training, sales, and development long enough to know how people appear when they're listening to someone. The times I got up and spoke, I saw that people had checked out. They were likely thinking about their own statements or the coming week. Nevertheless, for something that was supposed to encourage sister-like behavior, I felt hurt.

Taught first and then regularly encouraged, the activity that was most difficult for me was the bragging.

Throughout the weekends, every month, there would be pauses in the day and women were directed to arrive at a mic, or signal a previous graduate to pass the mic, and speak about whatever was braggable – including style, work accomplishments, relationships – and the audience would woot, clap, and celebrate it and the woman.

Before you think I am a heartless creature who cannot or will not find joy in others' deeds, please know that I am not like that. I am aware of and admire other people's accomplishments. By now, you've likely come to know that I didn't feel as though I had much to brag about; it's not in my nature to speak of my skills.

Feeling empty and believing I was weak rendered me devoid of any real interest in finding positive things about myself. I lacked the energy to share whatever I felt with hundreds of people. I was so frustrated with myself that unnecessary rancor applied to the women in the program. I perceived, and believed, that sisterhood is only powerful when everyone present chooses to act like sisters. I felt the following about the majority of these women:

- They were loud.
- They had no context for what I had been through, what I had done, what I was trying to do, and who I was.
- They were arrogant and self-important.

- They were trend-obsessed.
- They didn't know how to dress.
- They cared more about how they'd appear on social media than engaging with other women.

I'm certain that very few of the women were any of those things. **I made up a story, told it to myself, and believed it.**

I was candid in the early participant "what I need" survey, and it seemed that no one had read mine. When this program began, I did not have a full-time job, I wasn't in a romantic relationship, and I was stewing about the things I had tried to do since returning to New York. Whether or not the other women were interested in who I was and what I did, I was in a truly deep place of self-hatred.

By the time this program started, I expected myself to have figured out things; I was supposed to be working somewhere, to be in a healthy relationship, or at least one of those.

I was searching for, expecting, and needing affirmation, confirmation, and support while I struggled and when I succeeded. That's a lot to ask of a six month program.

I attended every month.
I refrained from bringing my full heart to the room.
I thought I was protecting myself.
Turns out I was resisting myself and everything I could have benefitted from and learned there.

To find success with consultants and coaches, **we must be open, willing, and ready to learn**. Was I open, willing, and ready to learn from them? I'd like to believe that I was. I certainly began there, and I wanted to get off the train almost right away.

What is *also* necessary when doing work with people that delves into the intimate portions of our minds and souls is **being aware of our triggers**. Triggers will trip us up and send us faster than Formula 1 to regret, resentment, and resistance.

In 2012, my triggers were exclusionary environments and conversations that seemed to happen around me. As much as I tried to engage with and learn about others, I was on the outside. I felt unwelcome. This likely occurred because I had become super sensitive to being different and apart from other people. While I was literally that for several months in 2009, I felt that way after my return to New York and for some time that followed. I knew this, and because I felt I had so much to make up for and I wanted to prevent being separate again, I tried harder than I should have.

I was supposed to be there.
I was supposed to participate.
I was supposed to be part of the crew.

Because I didn't actually believe that I belonged anywhere, I did one of two things:

- I made ridiculous efforts to be present for and with people, hoping to convince myself that I was welcome.
- I kept myself to myself, trying to convince my hard headed survivor self that being alone was not the same as being lonely because I chose to be on my own, and no one chooses to be lonely.

There are a few ways to repel people: one is trying too much, another is not trying at all.

When the program wrapped, I had met some nice people, two of whom are now friends, and I got to know a friend better. While it was not the experience I hoped it would be, it was an important step for me to get closer to accepting myself. I learned that if I feel something warrants a comment or my opinion, I need to answer two questions before I speak about it:

- **Am I judging, which is inappropriate, superficial, and unnecessary?**
- **Am I observing something or someone that provides an opportunity to learn?**

I also learned that you'll know when you're ready to make radical changes. For shock and awe to be effective, you can't force yourself into it.

14

WHO IS IMPORTANT.
WHY IS *MORE* IMPORTANT.

React:
I am really excited to help, contribute, and work as best as I can. I intend only to help. I'm empowered and fueled by instinct and faith (both acronyms, which are below here).
Act:
Give, write, make, assist, create, advocate, and go above and beyond with enthusiasm. Offer to help with unexpected and understaffed things.
Fact:
Remember that a having job cannot take the place of knowing who and what you want to be in the world. When it comes to doing things for others, focusing on "who" can make things fuzzy; the clarity is in the "why." With our "why," we can Design, Define, and Divine (copyright pending) everything.

Having survived a traumatic, potentially fatal, and life changing experience, I wake up grateful every single day. I believe that I always will. I was certainly doing this in 2012. And 2013. And 2014.

I remember waking up early and almost being overwhelmed by the sunrise and how the trees looked when the early spring weather turned them from leaf-bearing to bloom-growing. My gratitude for everything – because all of it almost wasn't mine to experience – extended to people. People I knew well, people I didn't know well, those I admired, folks I wanted to work with, work for, socialize with, date, and on and on. I had it in my mind that they were doing me a kindness, a favor really, by interacting with me. Hell, I don't know who I thought I was. I was a mess. I felt that I was:

Broken.
Not worth much.
Trading on luck.

What I actually was doing was stepping out on faith, for which there are two acronyms:
Float All Issues To Heaven, and
Fuck All Idiots That Hate.

While I was stepping out on faith I didn't accompany those actions with any real conviction. I may have been behaving and I was not believing.

For a while I bought two tickets to every concert, play, art exhibition, and the like. I picked up the check for meals. I paid for car rentals when going with people to places. Why? Could they not afford it? Nope. If my company wasn't a good enough reason, not having to pay for it was.

Doing work for free (or close to it).
Volunteering as though it was a paid job – always focused, dedicated, and available.
Asking for nothing.

Feeling guilty and weak for seeking clarity when directions weren't provided or were unclear.

Here's what I did not know or fully accept then:

REAL people – those who are ideal for you and your life – seek your company whether or not you pick up the check. They will like you, or they won't.

You do not *have* to do things for people.

I'd like to believe that I didn't apply and extend myself as much as I did in 2012, 2013, and 2014 with what I call the obligation motivation. In other words, doing something because I feel that I must is bad, wrong, and usually unhealthy. While there are exemptions to this, they are few and far between. I appreciate now why the vast number of people I once offered to help shooed me away. I also see why those who could benefit from my help in the short term took advantage of my offers.

Being genuine is a rare thing. By "genuine" I mean more than its literal definition. I mean not having a personal, self-serving agenda behind an offer of help.

I know a lot of people who perform, create, and produce. They express their needs and concerns, and I observed things that needed improvement, I believed in them, I liked them, and I could be of assistance. More times than I am comfortable admitting, I offered to help people with their tasks and projects.

A couple of them took me up on my offers. For a few months, work was done, plans were made, and products and projects were executed. I needed them far more than they needed me. It's not as though anyone said this, I just knew it. They may have known it too. Eventually, the project ended, the company dissolved, or I was removed from the organization. The big lesson here is one that I embraced fully in the fourth quarter of 2014:

Before anything happens, ask yourself why you want (or need) to do it.

- Did I feel that something was missing from my life and it could be found with or by others?
- How was this useful, valuable, or meaningful to me?
- What would doing the work, being part of the community/organization, and supporting the founders say about me?

Real talk: I woke up every morning with gratitude, yes, and complete disbelief that I was awake. I huffed and hustled to find things that justified my existence in the world because it cannot have been a random occurrence that I was alive. Making a difference in one way or another via useful activities justified my being on the Earth.

When I was growing up, it took me a little while to identify what it means to be "successful."

How I wanted to be known was never what society (read: my parents and those who were leadership in my life) defined. I remember to this day being asked in Kindergarten what I wanted to be when I grew up. I said, "I want to be an opera singer." (My father had just taken me to see The Metropolitan Opera (when it toured) perform "Hansel and Gretel" at the Hanna Theatre in Cleveland.)

I was nearly laughed out of the classroom. I didn't know enough about the world – or myself – to say that I wanted to be a nurse, an attorney, a teacher, an astronaut, a chef. I just knew that I loved music and I wanted to sing and share those stories and sounds with the world.

Why did I share that memory with you? To lay the groundwork for a lesson, a belief I came to know well when I was putting myself back together from 2009 until late 2014.

Fact: **Each of us gets to identify what we bring to the world and, as much as it is possible, *how* we can do this.**

What we can never forget is **we're doing this our own ways for our own reasons.**

While we are worth being acknowledged for our contributions to business, philanthropies, non-profits, causes, etc., those in charge have their own reasons for what they're doing and why. When we aren't treated with respect and appreciation, we must not take it personally.

I did not do any of the things shared in this book for credit, fame, or wealth. If the people I reported to were motivated by those factors more than I was, it ought not to have been a surprise when they ignored me, threw me under the bus, and saw me as a labor source and not as a person.

I needed to be honest with myself: why was I really offering to do work for people and not be paid, why was I actually putting in two or three days a week at a 501(C)(3)s as though I worked there, and why would I tolerate being treated like someone who didn't matter for as long as I did?

Because I had come to believe that I did not matter.

My worth was non-existent.

I still felt this way in 2013 when I offered to support a conference that was outside of New York. The organizers are terrific people: courageous, risk taking, and heart-driven. I think they were surprised that I offered, and they happily accepted. Of my own volition, I booked tickets, a car, and a room and arrived to set up. What I witnessed right away was that everyone else involved with this event worked for the company or lived in the event's city. I shook off the "there isn't a place for me" feeling before it took root and dived in to work. Long story short, as much as I may have done during that week, I was on the outside. The people who were local knew each other. The people who worked for and with the company knew each other. The ranks were closed, which I did not expect.

This is my truth: I was more excited about helping at the event than I had been about anything in the last couple of years. I believed in the organization, its purpose, and its founders. Everything was aligned with what I believed. I hoped that working for them could be the first step in a long-term involvement with the company. Did I say as much when I emailed my offer to help? No.

The timing was not right and my short-term intention was true – help at the conference. I hoped I was planting a seed and that they would see value in me. When the event had wrapped and the dust had settled, I hoped that we would talk about my being hired by the company.

During the conference, my actions were fueled by helping make the event better than the founders wanted and the participants expected. That was the right kind of fuel, because this week wasn't particularly enjoyable. I didn't dwell on that while I was there; there were tasks aplenty. While waiting for my flight home, I realized that everyone involved had different motivations and intentions. This was an important thing to recognize; it helped to steer me from a place I often spent time during my extended recovery. That's a place I call the **WDYDWS**: the **What Did You Do Wrong Swamp**.

Fact: if you do something wrong on someone else's time, in someone else's world, and for someone else's brand, they will tell you. They may not tell you right away (people are busy), they may not tell you as you'd like (specifically, directly) and they *will* tell you in one way or another.

The only interaction I have had with this team since the event is via email and my purchasing things they have published. And, that's okay. Why? I was only supposed to help them once. Our paths will cross again if we are to know each other.

In 2012, 2013, and 2014, I didn't have clear intentions when I lent myself, my skills, and my energy to companies, non-profits, and startups. I only had energy and eagerness, and a deep need to participate in something that wasn't mine; whatever it was had little or nothing to do with me. The work I did and the efforts invested during these months were not in any way weaker or less awesome because I was internally freaking out. At the time, though, **I was in these things partially because I was caught up in trying to prove my worth to myself.**

A couple of years ago someone asked me if I did volunteer work because I felt I owed the fact I wasn't killed to the universe. The question was daft. I have been active in social justice and community development since I was 15. I politely answered, "No. I've always done something like this. There is a need, I care, I can help, and so I do." Still, I have never forgotten the question and I reframed it when I decided to include this topic in the book.

The question I wish she had asked me is "Based on your vision of and hope for the world, how can you help shift what is needed in this organization?" *That* question speaks to my purpose, my "why."

And when you have your "why" it's much easier to find your "how" so you can execute.

As much as I worked (and as much as I may have been taken advantage of) I learned how to work in service in the healthiest, kindest, and truest ways. We create, do, and advocate for the product's buyer, the event attendee, the students and their families. The people you are reporting to are the "who." The people you serve are the "why."

Where you need to place focus is on the actual beneficiaries of what you're doing. They are the root of the important thing at play: the "why."

Our "why" is the foundation, the seed, the starting place of our legacy. When we have a "why" that is true and heartfelt, every single thing we create, support, and do will be better.

15

FACTS: WHAT I KNOW NOW AND WHAT I WILL ALWAYS KNOW

The chapters preceding this one provide what and how I felt (**React**), what I did (**Act**), and what I learned (**Fact**). This chapter includes facts. I encourage you apply your own context, experiences, and opinions to these and utilize them as needed.

The "self-help" genre came to be in the early 1980s. At most bookstores, you would find a range of books written by therapists, psychiatrists, and nutritionists. Many of these were half DIY therapy and half money grab. As the world and how people communicate, function, and thrive have evolved, there is still an audience for that method of informing.

This book has not been written that way because I am not that way.

Books about personal development, growth, and healing usually close with a positive "where I am now" chapter, because there was a journey to a destination and the author or subject arrived at that place.

I am still journeying.

I have worked at several different companies and for many people since the summer of 2009. While I believe that I did high quality work in all of those places, my effects no doubt improved as I became more conscious, clear, and self-believing. While the work was always top notch, I was not always at my best in those environments. My energy now matches my efforts. I am less reactive.

Before I commit to or agree to do something, I ask if it is aligned with the words I've chosen to live by for the year.

My words for 2017 were **Worth, Alliance, and Effect**.

I know that people are in my life to teach me something, to bring me joy, or both. And everything that happens is happening *for* me. Because I am still journeying. I still doubt, question, and wonder about the things that heart-driven humans deal with (weight, relationships, accomplishments). I wouldn't be human if I didn't do that.

Nine times out of ten, when we want to make change, we don't need to reinvent the wheel. Remember? We just have to polish the chromes and clean the rims.

Empathy is the secret sauce for everything.

I believe that **with candor we find clarity**.
I feel that being super truthful is the most helpful
I know that when we stop learning, we stop living.

I am still grateful every morning to wake up.
I appreciate everything, including my own desires, abilities, and actions.

I am a soldier goddess.

This journey is for my life. And this is the way it's supposed to be.

What follows here are my overall takeaways, the lessons I picked up since 2009.

Most of these are connected to or are an extension of one of the chapters.
May they serve you as needs arise.
May you find *your* happy and always live there.

- **Don't *look* for work. Look for an experience, a movement, and people.** [Chapters 8, 9, and 12, 14]
  - Finding the work you want and need can be easier than you think.
  - Ask yourself these questions:
    - What are your gifts?
    - Who needs them?
    - What solutions can you provide?
    - What do you enjoy doing?
    - What have you done that has become native to, or rooted in, you?
  - Answer these honestly. Watch the opportunities appear.

- **Don't be in judgment; be in observation.** [Chapter 13]
  - Is there real value in opining about other people?
  - Is there any value in expressing said opinion?
  - Does what people do, say, or wear really affect you?
  - Can you learn from what they're doing?
  - Can anyone learn from it?

- **Some things can only be learned by actually doing them.** [Every chapter]
    - Reading about something is informative; it's not truly experiential.
    - When you do it, you *really* learn it; it becomes embedded.

- **Repetition reads like desperation. Both can be (and generally are) repellent.** [Chapters 5, 6, 10, 11, and 14]
    - The brands that produce the best cars, bags, shoes, etc. don't push and push and push the public to buy them.
    - The designers and producers know that these items are worth what they cost.
    - Regarding your own work, *you* are *worth* what you charge.
    - You are worth spending time with.
    - You are worth whatever dedicated time and energy you require.
        - Trust and believe in these truths and in yourself.

- **Intention and perception do not always play nice, align, or jibe**. [Chapters 10 and 13]
    - There are a couple of ways you can level the playing field here:
        - If someone looks perplexed or responds with something that's unrelated or counter to what you said, ask what they heard.
        - If they did not understand or receive what you said, reset and reframe your statements.

- **Don't be sarcastic in emails or text messages.** [Chapter 10]
  - In the absence of a tone of voice or any facial expressions, what you mean may not be what someone perceives.
  - While you may feel that you're being obvious, if you feel that you've been disconnecting, especially if you haven't spoken to or seen someone in a while, be as candid and as emotional as you feel you need to be.
  - When you are *truly* expressive, know and trust that people will believe what you intend.

- **Give before you get (if that feels like the right order for you)**. [Chapter 14]
  - A reason for doing things can certainly be that help is needed and you are able to provide something. Read: no agenda.
  - So long as the action is aligned with your purpose and you want to do something, you will learn.
  - And, learning is a good form of payment.

- **Asking "What do I want?" and answering it truly and from your heart as much as from your mind is one of the most important things you can do in life.** [Chapters 6, 8, 9, 13, and 14]
  - Once I knew what I wanted, I was able to get it.
  - Once you *honestly* know it, you will find all sorts of ways to get it.
  - Answer simply. Trust the first thing that comes to mind.
  - Here are my answers, from the first time I asked myself for real "What do I want?" in early summer, 2016:

    - I want to sleep through the night and wake up the next day looking forward to the day, not just feel grateful to be awake.
    - I want to laugh.
    - I want to sing.
    - I want to write.
    - I want to make things better for the people I love and people who are in need.
    - I want to live a meaningful life.
    - I want to be at peace with who I am and how I am.

- **Worth. If there is anything for you to own and live by it's this.**
  - Worth is always within you, whether you acknowledge, feel, and believe it or not.
  - It's like Daylight Savings: always there.

- **There is no need to rush.**
  - Things don't happen on time; they happen in time (copyright pending).

- **Chances are, no one is on the same path as you.**
  - You've chosen your path (your way of dealing with something).
  - How you "walk" it is up to you.
  - While you're journeying, especially after a trauma, be open to who you will encounter.
  - They could share with you what is important and meaningful to them.

- **Everything in life can come back to us with the exception of time. Time is the most valuable thing in life.** [Introduction and every chapter]

- **We are here, and that is everything.**

APPENDIX

Among the things that helped me, empowered me, and/or made me smile during my official and unofficial recoveries are these books, people, and programs.

- The Gifts of Imperfection by Brené Brown
- The Art of Non-Conformity: Set Your Own Rules, Live The Life You Want, and Change the World by Chris Guillebeau
- What To Do When It's Your Turn by Seth Godin
- The Art of Being Unmistakable by Srinivas Rao
- The War of Art: Break Through the Blocks and Win Your Inner Creative Battles by Steven Pressfield
- God Never Blinks: 50 Lessons for Life's Little Detours by Regina Brett
- Do You! 12 Laws to Access the Power in You to Achieve Happiness and Success by Russell Simmons with Chris Morrow
- The Game of Life for Women and how to play it by Florence Scovel Shinn
- Love is a Mixtape: Life and Loss, One Song at a time by Rob Sheffield
- Help, Thanks, Wow: Three Essential Prayers by Anne Lamott

- Kid President's Guide to Being Awesome by Robby Novak and Brad Montague
- The Way of the Brave Bear: Speak Up, Stand Out. Change Your World by Berni Xiong

- SynchroDestiny Course, online at The Chopra Center
- Leadership & Listening Institute at Her Life, Her Legacy by Theresa Campbell
- Realign+SHINE - Clinical Hypnotherapy with Karla Lightfoot

As I said in the Introduction, I wrote this book to provide actionable things for people so they can effectively deal with crises and challenges. If you have a question, want to arrange a speaking engagement, or talk about stuff, you are welcome to get in touch.

If you want to know literally, specifically, and personally what something meant to me and why, I am happy to share that with you.

You can reach me via my website, KateHarvie.com (you can email me from the Contact page), or get in touch directly on kate@kateharvie.com.

ACKNOWLEDGEMENTS

To say it takes a village when it comes to rebuilding and resetting after my traumatic brain injury is an understatement. I literally could not have done it without the presence and contributions of the people included here.

While some of these people and I are no longer in touch, I appreciate what every one of them did for my family and me, and what all of them do today.

Thank you.

Angela Taormino, Alison Bartolone Gill, Jonathan Gill, Michael Bartolone, Alison Ritz, Zena Itani, Chrysanthy Pelekanos, Deno Angelopolous, Holger Roëhl, Lorraine Debose, Lex Federbush, Marjorie Federbush, Elizabeth DiAlto, Ernie Vasquez, the entire 2009 Sephora US corporate and store staff, the staff at NYU Langone Hospital-Brooklyn, the staff at Mount Sinai Hospital, Samone Weissman, Mabel Peralta, Yi Jia Frye, Ivan Santelises, Margaret Slattery, Bill Slattery, Andrew M. Byrne, Michael Hrostoski, Francesca Alexander, Heather Polyi, Shaun Rowan, Miguel Martinez, Daniele Filippello, Kenny Ramos, Oscar Manuel Cardona, Anthony Paul, Frantz Desir, Yardena Hipsh, Riley Temple, Kimberly Anderson, Randy Davis, Peter Hay Halpert, Dr. Eric Baud, Myriam Altieri-Haslinger, Lute Quintrell, Lynn Quintrell, Dr. Steven Lacey, Kathy Lacey, Elizabeth Lacey, PhD, Lorelei Stein-Sapir, Jim Grumbine, Jason Revilla,

Cyndi Clark, Catherine Somoza, Corinne Edwards, John LaPorte, A.J. Leon, Melissa Leon, Bryonn Bain, Carol Dakin, Thomas Dale, Christopher Preston Thompson, Sherrie Fell, Cyrena Esposito, Becky Barzal, Alison Raffaele Tatem, Salma Gibara, Sam Gibara, Steve Marden, Justin Foster, Stella Grizont, Diane Marazzi, Richard Tembo, Alex Twersky, Nikki Mirasola, George Del Barrio, Trudy Appling, Chanz Simmons, Catherine Else, Janet Wall, Dr. Ming Zeng, Dr. Anousheh Benegar, Eric T. Wagner, Emily DiCicco, Irene Pappas, Ken Mercer, Kathy Coleman, Kathy O'Neill, Marshay Mitchell, Jon Giganti, Amy Lynn Koskē, Denise Gvardian, Dave Builta, Oksana Mirzakandova, Marianne Manthey, Aaron Stinnette, John Spinhirne, Katie Shames, Catherine Kay, Carrianne DeMicoli, Siraaj Muhammad, Michelle Muhammad, Brian Sheppard, Todd Carpenter, Chris Roberti, Joan Kim, Neil Kernis, Bushra Khan, Skye Suttie, Vilma Schonwetter, Dena Netterville, Wil Velazquez, Ellen Lee Maurer, Michael Riscica, Mario Hardy, Samantha Park, Peter Darbey, Jr., Hanif Peters-Davis, Tony Moore, Scheron Williams, Kwame Garrett-Price, John McCoy, Becki McCoy, Jill Harrington, Dr. Nancy Rosen, Natalie Thomas, Dr. Anthony Hayek, Dr. Robert Maciunas, Dr. James Sisler, Dr. Marcella Allen, Bonnie Frankel, Caroline Werner, Patricia Chilcott, Barb Closen, Brand Closen, Christine Breuker, John Breuker, Howard Steindler, Terri Steindler, Jim Halloran, Leslie Halloran, Ingrid Luders, Dr. Hans Luders, David Warshawsky, Lee Warshawsky, Ruthie Fiordalis, Vincent Fiordalis, Alan Fossler, Elizabeth Carroll, Travis Smith, Dr. Vikki Johnson, Rev. Susan Sparks, Rev. Dr. Cheryl Dudley, Karen Taylor-Bass, William McClelland, Andrea Clark, Theresa Campbell, Jamie Sammons, Janet Wall, Jamie Lord, Hillary Lord, Berni Xiong, Aaron Bashirian, Arash Haile, Abraham Cajudo, Eric Devon Bass, Amy Pawlicki, Avi Markowski, Dr. Beth Leeman-Markowski, Rayan Parikh, Brian Merlo, Tim Intagliata, David Melendez, Raheem

Taylor, Vivian Schodowski, Mary Walker Sprunt, Romulo Vinhaes, Anthony Lewis, Renford Dunn, Asia Gregg, Dr. Christopher Stepien, Eugene Friesen, Sam Hubert, Kevin Fannin, Turner Roach, Peter Udeshi, Meghan Smerick, Chuck Smerick, Deb Smerick, Ashleigh Smerick, Zach Smerick, Josh Smerick, Jennifer Elliott, Mike Sheehan, Carol Wolf, Christine Manoli, Gerard Manoli, Karla Lightfoot, Larry Isard, Susan Bai, Mary Ward, Miriam Greene, Jake Heider, Jennifer Jett, Christian Burns, Tauhir Jones, Angus Brewer, Yashana McCauley-Parrish, Laura Filancia, James Eller, Aileen Sexton Kopfinger, Yulian Ramos, Lisa Blair, Pete Harman, Diana Harman, Dr. James Dooley, Debbie Groby, Amanda Harvie, Teddy Harvie, Chris Lord, Iris Harvie, Tom Harvie, and Ted Harvie.

ABOUT THE AUTHOR

Kate Harvie was born to teach people how to tell their stories. She does this with writing, editing, marketing, brand strategy, and development online and offline. A graduate of law school, she is a startup founder and advocate for survivors of all kinds of trauma.

A published writer for online magazines (BeautyNewsNYC), print publications (West End Word), blogs (L.M. Durand), and the company where she works as a community manager (Suit & Artist), Kate began in advertising at FutureBrand's digital practice. She worked at INTAGLIA HOME COLLECTION in St. Louis in marketing and sales. She co-wrote curricula, vodcast scripts, and training dialogues at Sephora and for several cosmetic companies. As the community and content manager at The Phat Startup, she was responsible for the website's content creation, editing, and ghostwriting. She works in communications and strategic planning for The Vanderbilt Republic.

Kate is a survivor of a traumatic brain injury. That is the impetus for her first book. She is a singer, a volunteer at non-profits and entrepreneurial programs around the country, and the person you want in your corner and on your speed dial.

www.KateHarvie.com